DEVELOPING YOUR

Spiritual

UNDERSTANDING

1st Edition

DEVELOPING YOUR

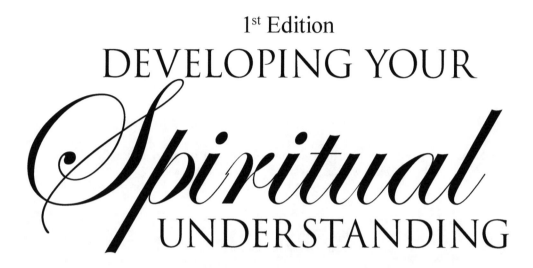

Spiritual

UNDERSTANDING

*"The role of the church is to meet people where
they are regardless of who they are."*

TEACHER'S YOUTH CONFIRMATION MANUAL

authorHOUSE®

AuthorHouse™ LLC
1663 Liberty Drive
Bloomington, IN 47403
www.authorhouse.com
Phone: 1-800-839-8640

Published by AuthorHouse   02/22/2014

ISBN: 978-1-4918-4159-4 (sc)
ISBN: 978-1-4918-4160-0 (e)

Any people depicted in stock imagery provided by Thinkstock are models,
and such images are being used for illustrative purposes only.
Certain stock imagery © Thinkstock.

This book is printed on acid-free paper.

Because of the dynamic nature of the Internet, any web addresses or links contained in this book may have changed
since publication and may no longer be valid. The views expressed in this work are solely those of the author and do
not necessarily reflect the views of the publisher, and the publisher hereby disclaims any responsibility for them.

Request for permission should be addressed in writing to:
REW Ministries
P.O. Box 571831
Las Vegas, NV 89157

For additional information visit:
www.REWMinistries.org

Email: pastor@rewministries.org
or call: (702) 875- 5957

Cover design by Tom Smith

Disclaimer

Materials used for the confirmation classes are not intended to replace any literature printed and approved by any church denomination.

DEVELOPING YOUR SPIRITUAL UNDERSTANDING (DYSU)

By Ralph E. Williamson, D. Min.

Table of Contents

INTRODUCTION

Jurgen Moltmann reminds us in his book, The Way of Jesus Christ "Salvation is an entity which includes the wholeness and well-being of human beings, Salvation is for the totus homo; it is not merely salvation of soul for the individual. Salvation does not mean merely 'spiritual benefits'. It includes the health of the body." It is by faith and the power of the gospel that human freedom can be obtained through salvation which reunites an individual with the family of God and their Creator.

In this context the church serves as a change agent that promotes a resounding message of God's love and ultimate desire to be in relationship with humanity, to bring about redemption, wholeness, and salvation. This love of God permeates through time and space, from generation to generation, from the beginning to the end of time. It is an everlasting love that will never lose its power. As a change agent, the church has a spiritual, moral, and social responsibility toward its community and to fallen man, to introduce to some and reintroduce to others a God who controls what Niebuhr depicts as "the nature and destiny of man."

As God commanded the Israelites in (Deuteronomy 4:9; Deuteronomy 6:6-7; Deuteronomy 11:18-19), to take seriously their spiritual responsibility, both the parent and the church today has that same responsibility to teach, train and instruct their children in the same manner. The scripture is very clear when we *Train a child in the way he should go, and when he is old he will not turn from it.* (Proverbs 22:6).

Many youth today are looking for answers and solutions that provide hope, happiness, and success. The challenge of the 21st century church is to provide them with positive alternatives and guidance that encourage and place value on their spiritual development. Youth are constantly inundated with negative influences that create the inability for them to make sound decisions. Illegal drugs, gang activity, teen-age pregnancy, parental divorce, sexual transmitted disease, bullying, suicide and murder, are just a few of the challenges that can impact their way of life.

The focus of the confirmation lessons is for youth to become knowledgeable about their faith traditions and beliefs, and the importance of having a relationship with God and our Lord and Savior Jesus Christ. Each lesson is written to educate youth on some of the standard doctrines of the church, Christian Apologetics and building relationships in the 21st century.

PURPOSE

The purpose of the confirmation process is more than teaching youth about the Bible and their Christian belief system. The purpose is three-fold: (1) Increase youth confidence; (2) Encourage active youth participation in the church, school, community and the world; and (3) Teach youth how to make sound Christian decisions.

In every Christian community it is the shared responsibility of parents/guardians, the pastor and church membership to educate youth on spiritual principles that influence making the right moral decisions. Throughout the course, value will be placed on youth concerns and issues that impact their lives while providing spiritual guidance. The course will also assist youth with biblical answers and solutions to many of life's problems. In the process, youth will become empowered with a renewed sense of confidence and self-esteem when given the right tools to make spiritual life choices. Each lesson was purposely developed to aid youth with understanding their Christian belief and how to share their faith with relatives and friends.

"...You are a part of the body of Christ.
God has chosen different ones in the church to do his work."
1 Corinthians 12:27-28

xi

The intended goal and purpose during the next several weeks:

- **Prepare** youth with confidence when using the Bible to access scriptures for every aspect of their life.
  - *Keep this Book of the Law always on your lips; meditate on it day and night, so that you may be careful to do everything written in it. Then you will be prosperous and successful.* **(Joshua 1:8)**
- **Empower** youth with the knowledge of the Word of God.
  - *For the word of God is alive and active. Sharper than any double-edged sword, it penetrates even to dividing soul and spirit, joints and marrow; it judges the thoughts and attitudes of the heart.* **(Hebrews 4:12)**
- **Transform** youth into becoming a disciple of Christ by demonstrating the importance of supporting one another and working together in small groups.
  - *I am the vine; you are the branches. If a man remains in me and I in him, he will bear much fruit; apart from me you can do nothing.* **(John 15:5)**

Each lesson was specifically developed to create an opportunity for youth to work together with other youth in a small group setting. In this 21st century, as a youth they need to know that they are not just a member of a local church, but a citizen of the world. The role as a young citizen is to help one another build strong working relationships in their church, school, community and world.

OVERVIEW

Preparing for the Workshops

1. Identify the program administrator.
   a. The administrator should become familiar with the lessons
   b. Select instructor(s) if necessary
   c. Both administrator and instructor(s) are to review the lesson plans together
2. Three weeks prior to the start of the confirmation classes, a letter will be mailed to parents/ guardians. The letter will contain the date, time, place and lesson outlines for the nine weeks.
3. The estimated time for each class is two-hours.
4. The confirmation information will be posted in the church bulletin(s) and on the church website. The posting will be for three consecutive Sundays prior to the start of the confirmation lessons. (The allotted time is necessary to generate parental support and youth participation.)
5. A registration card and folder will be developed for each participant prior to the first confirmation class. The folder will contain a confirmation schedule and Questionnaire I.
6. The use of a New International Version (NIV) Youth Study Bible will be used in conjunction with each lesson.

Confirmation Classes

Each lesson should begin with the recommended opening song written by Israel & New Breed, "I Am Not Forgotten" followed with a prayer and scripture chosen especially for each lesson. The instructor will separate youth into small groups of 5-7 individuals. Each group should have a good

xii

"…You are a part of the body of Christ.
God has chosen different ones in the church to do his work."
1 Corinthians 12:27-28

mix of both male and female participants. If possible, try separating youth who know each other. The intent of the confirmation process is to emphasize:

- the value of collaborating with others in small groups
- developing positive relationships
- making Christian decisions

Lesson Summary:

Lesson I—Understanding Confirmation

The lesson will discuss the following topics:
- Defining Confirmation
- Building Community
- Confirmation Goal
- Your Decision on Becoming a Disciple of Christ

(This lesson will also include a questionnaire. The objective of the questionnaire is to provide the instructor with valuable insight of each youth's knowledge, attitudes, beliefs, values and behavior.)

Lesson II—The Trinity

The lesson is designed to give biblical references that will provide youth with a better understanding of God in three persons.
- What is meant by the Trinity
- God the Father

Lesson III—Jesus Christ Is Lord

The lesson will focus on the various aspects of Jesus.

- Jesus is the Son of God
- Jesus is the Christ
- Jesus is the Savior of the World

Lesson IV—The Holy Spirit

The lesson will highlight the third part of the Trinity.
- What is the Holy Spirit
- Life in the Spirit
- Fruit of the Spirit

Lesson V—Salvation

The lesson will focus on the importance of Salvation.
- What is Salvation

"…You are a part of the body of Christ.
God has chosen different ones in the church to do his work."
1 Corinthians 12:27-28

xiii

Lesson VI—Worship

The lesson was developed to help youth understand how we worship in our daily lives, in church and community.
- Defining Worship
- Where We Worship
- The Way We Worship
- How We Worship

Worship Terms and Definition

Lesson VII

Lesson Summary:
- The Bible
- The Books of the Old Testament
- The Books of the New Testament
- What I Believe
- The General Confession

Lesson VIII

- The Mission
- Statements of Faith
- My Responsibility
- Final Questionnaire
- Preparation for Confirmation Service (See Handout-13)

"...You are a part of the body of Christ.
God has chosen different ones in the church to do his work."
1 Corinthians 12:27-28

Special Instructions

It is important that youth take this confirmation process seriously. All information provided in the lessons is important. No part of the confirmation process is optional. Youth attendance is vital. Each youth must make a personal decision to be regular in attendance. When youth make the decision to be a part of this confirmation process, they will experience the power of the Holy Spirit working in their life like never before.

It is proven that journaling helps to enhance our learning, understanding and center our thoughts upon those things that lend value to our lives. Journaling is a tool that allows us to portray our thoughts and personal feeling, freeing our mind for reflection at a later time. In every sector of society corporate and world leaders, educators and the average person all keep a personal journal.

- Youth are encouraged to keep a journal following each confirmation lesson. Their journal should reflect an honest summary of their personal feelings as a result of the lesson material presented. Youth are also encouraged to highlight scripture references to help their future development in Bible study and with their daily meditation.
- Do not use individuals' names. Assign a number to each youth. This number will be placed on Questionnaire I, Final Questionnaire.
- Divide students into small groups of 5-7. The groups will remain intact throughout the entire confirmation series. The group experience will help students understand the importance of working together and building a spiritual community.
- Appropriate breaks should be given during each class. The first and each proceeding class will open with a prayer and the confirmation goal.

Materials

Each youth is to receive:

- New International Version (NIV) Youth Study Bible
- Pen
- Highlighters
- Paper
- Handouts and questionnaires
- Magazines and newspapers

"...You are a part of the body of Christ.
God has chosen different ones in the church to do his work."
1 Corinthians 12:27-28

XV

LESSON I

UNDERSTANDING
CONFIRMATION

Lesson I—Understanding Confirmation
Opening Song: I Am Not Forgotten

Prayer: Heavenly Father, Creator and Giver of every good and perfect gift, we acknowledge that You are awesome! You are all powerful. We know that all wisdom and knowledge comes from You. Bless us with a desire to receive all You have to offer. Amen.

Scripture: *Now you are the body of Christ, and each one of you is a part of it . . .* **(1 Corinthians 12:27)**

Lesson Summary:
- Defining Confirmation
- Building Community
- Confirmation Goals
- Decision on Becoming a Disciple of Christ

(This lesson will include a questionnaire. The objective of the questionnaire is to provide the instructor with valuable insight of the youth's knowledge, attitudes, beliefs, values and behavior.)

What is Confirmation?

1. Confirmation is another way of saying we confirm our faith belief. It is the act of verifying or confirming what we have been taught by our parents and our church as it relates to God and our relationship with Christ Jesus.
2. In our faith tradition, many of us were baptized long before we had the opportunity to understand the meaning of our baptism.

   When we were baptized, our parents or guardians took a vow and agreed to accept the responsibility to see that we were taught the nature and the meaning of our baptism.

The church also stood in agreement to help teach us such things as the Lord's Prayer, the Ten Commandments, the meaning of our Christian faith and all the things a Christian should know.

3. We believe that baptism is a sacrament ordained of Christ. Our baptism is not only a profession of our faith, it is also a sign of God's grace and good will towards us.
4. Confirmation is about a personal acceptance and acknowledgment of God's grace and love for us through the free gift of salvation through Jesus Christ.

The Bible tells us, "God so loved the world that he gave his One and Only Son." **(John 3:16 NIV)** As a result of God's gift to the world, our parents or guardians accepted the gift of Christ for us on the day we were baptized.

Although the gift is free, we have the right to accept it or to reject it. Confirmation gives us that opportunity to make the decision and decide for ourselves if we want this gift from God and to "confirm" what was accepted for us by our parents, guardians and the church.

5. As youth, we are now at the age where we can decide for ourselves about our salvation.
6. While our parents and the church will be there to help and guide us along this journey, it is now our responsibility and God requires each of us to make our own decision.

"...You are a part of the body of Christ.
God has chosen different ones in the church to do his work."
1 Corinthians 12:27-28

3

7. We are more mentally prepared to comprehend and learn what it means to be a Christian and active member of the body of Christ. We are also old enough to learn what we believe: our doctrine, discipline, history, heritage and how we are to live as Christians.

8. While we may not have the answers to all the questions, with God on our side and the Spirit of the Lord to guide us, we can learn along the way.

9. We are old enough where others will know we made a decision for ourselves and were confirmed before God and the church in what we believe. Our confirmation gives us an active voice where we can now live out our faith in our church, school, community and the world.

Building Community

In this ever-changing environment, it is imperative for youth to recognize the value in having positive relationships with those who will help them make the right spiritual choices. During the next several weeks youth will have the opportunity to build their own Christian community by interacting and engaging with their peers in small groups. Youth are to work together on selected projects to enhance their knowledge of the Christian faith.

My Confirmation Goal

(The confirmation goal should be read and recited by students during each confirmation class.)

My Christian journey thus far has been one that was decided for me as a child. I am no longer a child. I am now at the age where I must decide if I want to accept God's free gift of salvation and make it my own.

My parents, guardians and church are here to help and guide me along this journey. However, the decision is now my responsibility. The instructions I receive during my confirmation classes will help me learn more about my faith. While I am in the process of learning about my faith and how to be a Christian, I will not pretend to know all the answers. I am willing to learn all I can and to be all I can. I will give back to my church. I will live out my faith in my school, community and the world.

As a responsible youth, my confirmation will give me the opportunity to become an active member of the church body.

My profession of faith will also allow the Holy Spirit to begin a new work in me and confirm me into the church. I affirm that my confirmation goal is to live out what my parents, guardians and church have accepted for me as an infant.

"...You are a part of the body of Christ.
God has chosen different ones in the church to do his work."
1 Corinthians 12:27-28

Your Decision on Becoming a Disciple of Christ

1.	During this confirmation process, you will have a unique opportunity to make a decision to become a disciple of Christ. When the invitation is given, it is our hope that you will respond and be confirmed on Confirmation Sunday.
2.	You do not have to be confirmed. The decision will be entirely yours. You may decide now or at a later time. However, it is our hope that you will accept the invitation to Christian discipleship at the time of confirmation. Choosing not to be confirmed does not affect your ability to participate in the church or in any activities at your church.
3.	If you have been baptized, we affirm your baptism and there is no need to be re-baptized.
4.	If you have not been baptized, you will be given an opportunity to be baptized following your response to accept Jesus Christ as your Lord and Savior. Baptism is the gateway into the body of Christ, a particular denomination and local church.
5.	Confirmation is done with your confession and a prayer that the Holy Spirit will continue to work in your life. If you choose to be confirmed, you will become an active member of the body of Christ with all rights and privileges to the kingdom of God.
6.	While you may complete these classes, confirmation is not the end. It is the beginning of a lifelong journey together with the Lord. Confirmation will build on the values your parents have taught you, what you have learned in the church and your personal experiences with God.
7.	Our prayer is that you will take this confirmation process seriously. Everything in these classes is important. "No part is optional, your attendance is vital." You must make a decision to be regular in attendance. When you make this decision, you will experience the power of the Holy Spirit working in your life like never before.
8.	When you are confirmed, you are making a public profession before your family, church and friends that you are now a part of the body of Christ!

"...You are a part of the body of Christ.
God has chosen different ones in the church to do his work."
1 Corinthians 12:27-28

5

Questionnaire I (circle one answer for each question)

Gender_____ Student#_____ Age_____

1. How would you use your knowledge to explain to a non-believer that the Bible is the true and inspired Word of God?
   a. God chose angels to translate in every language what He wanted us to know and learn.
   b. All Scripture is God-breathed and is useful for teaching, rebuking, correcting and training in righteousness.[1]
   c. In the beginning of time God sat down and wrote every word and gave them to us to read.

2. If you knew your best friend was about to make a wrong decision, how would you use your Christian beliefs, knowledge and values to help your friend?
   a. Ask your pastor to pray for them
   b. Invite them to a Christian movie
   c. By demonstrating the fruit of the spirit

3. Explain how having knowledge about the Bible would be helpful in your own spiritual development.
   a. Reading my Bible every day, especially on Sundays before I go to church.
   b. It helps me to understand Christ Jesus our Lord, His life, birth, death, resurrection and God's plan of salvation.
   c. It has great stories of people who lived in the past.

4. Tim is into drugs and gang activity. Explain how you would lead Tim to Christ.
   a. Show Tim why we need Jesus in our lives and in the world.
   b. Tell Tim if he continues doing wrong he will most likely get in trouble and go to jail.
   c. Convince Tim that if he does not stop, you will have to report him to his parents.

5. Explain how your knowledge about salvation, faith and baptism would help someone struggling with depression and poor self esteem.
   a. Tell them about the power of positive thinking.
   b. Give advice on how to dress and act so people will like them.
   c. Explain how confirmation works.

6. Explain how different styles of music enhances the church service and church growth.
   a. It encourages others to praise God and allows people to sing, dance and pray in various ways.
   b. Worship should not have to change to make the church grow.
   c. The pastor in charge, not the music, determines the need for church growth.

7. Explain why your involvement in a ministry that helps the poor and the homeless would be important for your spiritual growth.
   a. Involvement in a ministry does not impact spiritual growth.

   Involvement in a ministry helps to serve out of love and gratitude for what God has done for each of us. c. Spiritual growth is only measured by how much you know about the Bible.

8. Explain the Trinity
   a. The Trinity is when you have three of the same things.
   b. The Trinity is God in three different persons.
   c. The Trinity is the three aspects or personas of God.

"...You are a part of the body of Christ.
God has chosen different ones in the church to do his work."
1 Corinthians 12:27-28

REW
MINISTRIES

Personal Journal

Take time to reflect and write about what you learned in this lesson as it relates to "What is Confirmation and Becoming a Disciple of Christ."

Below are a few reminders from lesson 1 to assist with your personal journal writing:

- While I am in the process of learning about my faith and how to be a Christian, I will not pretend to know all the answers.
- I am willing to learn all I can, to be all I can.
- I promise to give back to my church.
- I will live out my faith in my school, community, and the world.

Prayer:

Gracious God, I pray and thank you for this opportunity and the abundant life you have afforded me as a youth. Prepare me with confidence when using the bible to access scripture for every aspect of my life. Empower me with the knowledge of Your Word. Transform my life into becoming a disciple of Christ. Amen.

"...You are a part of the body of Christ.
God has chosen different ones in the church to do his work."
1 Corinthians 12:27-28

7

Personal Journal:

Summarize what you have learned in this lesson.

_____

_____

_____

_____

_____

_____

_____

_____

_____

_____

How will this lesson impact your life?

_____

_____

_____

_____

_____

_____

_____

_____

_____

_____

_____

"...You are a part of the body of Christ.
God has chosen different ones in the church to do his work."
1 Corinthians 12:27-28

LESSON II

THE TRINITY GOD IN THREE PERSONS

Lesson II—The Trinity

Opening Song: I am not forgotten

Prayer: We open our hearts to You dear God. Give us wisdom and understanding. Guide and teach us in knowledge and in truth. Create within us a spirit and a desire to learn Your purpose for our lives and to grow stronger in our faith. Amen.

Scripture: *Consequently, you are no longer foreigners and aliens, but fellow citizens with God's people and members of God's household, built on the foundation of the apostles and prophets, with Christ Jesus himself as the chief cornerstone. In him the whole building is joined together and rises to become a holy temple in the Lord. And in him you too are being built together to become a dwelling in which God lives by his Spirit.* **(Ephesians 2:19-22)**

Lesson Summary
*   What is meant by the Trinity?

Principle Teaching: What is meant by the Trinity: God as Father, Son and Holy Spirit?

Material Needed:
*   Easels, paper, pen, highlighters, magic markers
*   NIV Youth Study Bibles
*   Handout 7—God Is

Special Instructions: Students are encouraged to highlight scripture references in their Bibles and to keep a personal journal. For each group exercise, divide students into small groups of 5-7.

My Confirmation Goal

My Christian journey thus far has been one that was decided for me as a child. I am no longer a child. I am now at the age where I must decide if I want to accept God's free gift of salvation and make it my own.

My parents, guardians and church are here to help and guide me along this journey. However, the decision is now my responsibility. The instructions I receive during my confirmation classes will help me learn more about my faith.

While I am in the process of learning about my faith and how to be a Christian, I will not pretend to know all the answers. I am willing to learn all I can and to be all I can. I will give back to my church. I will live out my faith in my school, community and the world.

As a responsible youth, my confirmation will give me the opportunity to become an active member of the church body.

My profession of faith will allow the Holy Spirit to begin a new work in me and confirm me into the church. I affirm that my confirmation goal is to live out what my parents, guardians and church have accepted for me as an infant when I was baptized.

What Is Meant By The Trinity?

The Trinity is defined as the three personas of God. **(See Handout 7—the Trinity)**
*   God the Father
*   God the Son
*   God the Holy Spirit

"...You are a part of the body of Christ.
God has chosen different ones in the church to do his work."
1 Corinthians 12:27-28

11

Exercise I

This exercise is designed to give youth biblical references that will help educate them with a better understanding of what is meant by the Trinity, the three personas of God.

While reading the following aloud, have the students look up and highlight each of the below scriptures in their New International Version (NIV) Youth Study Bible. **(20 minutes)**

The word "Trinity" does not appear in the Bible; it was created by scholars. Throughout the Bible, God is presented as being Father, Son, and Holy Spirit, not three "gods", but three personas of the One and Only God. **(see Matthew 28:19)**

All three are a tri-unity, inhabiting one another and working together to accomplish the divine design in the universe.[2] **(see John 16:13-15)**

The Scriptures present the Father as the source of creation, the giver of life and God of all the universe.

- Genesis1:1-31; 2:1
- John 1:1-3
- 1 Corinthians 8:6
- Ephesians 3:14-15
- Hebrews 1:1-2

The Son is depicted as the image of the invisible God in human form. The Son is the exact representation of God's being and nature, the Messiah and Redeemer.

- John 1:14
- Philippians 2:5-6
- Colossians 1:15-16
- Hebrews 1:3

The Spirit is God in action, God reaching people—influencing, regenerating, infilling and guiding humankind.

- John 14:26
- John 16:13-15
- Acts 2:2-4

Exercise II

Have the students do the following exercise. Read the exercise to the students.

1. Which symbol would best describe the Trinity?
   a. Circle
   b. Square
   c. Triangle

2. With the symbol you have selected, draw a diagram that shows how the Father, Son and Holy Spirit are connected as one. **(3 minutes)**

Handout

Provide the students with Handout 7—the Trinity after the exercises are completed.

"...You are a part of the body of Christ.
God has chosen different ones in the church to do his work."
1 Corinthians 12:27-28

God the Father

- God is the first part of the Trinity Youth will discuss in a small group who God is. Youth are to use only short word phrases to describe God. The instructor will choose a volunteer to list the youth responses on easel paper. Their responses will be helpful in completing the small group exercise below. **(10 minutes)**

Exercise III (Small Group)

The instructor will read the following to the groups: In *Claim the Name Confirmation* book written by Crystal A. Zinkiewicz, youth are told, "God is behind all, above all, beyond all, and within all, God is the source of all there is, God is the sustaining power of the universe and God is present with us . . ."[3]

Instructions

Part I

- Divide students into their small groups. Have students look up the scriptures listed below in their NIV Youth Study Bible to help complete this assignment.
  - Psalm 7:11
  - 1 Corinthians 10:13
  - Hebrews 3:4
  - 2 Chronicles 30:9
  - Psalm 54:4
  - Daniel 9:9
  - 2 Samuel 22:3
  - Job 36:5
  - Deuteronomy 4:24
  - Psalm 84:11

Part II

- Youth are to write out the scripture with the entire verse that best identifies who God is on Handout 8—God Is.

The ten scriptures in the bible that identify who God is:

Teacher's answers below:

- God is a righteous judge.
  (Psalm 7:11)
- God is faithful. **(1 Corinthians 10:13)**
- God is the builder of everything.
  (Hebrews 3:4)
- God is gracious and compassionate.
  (2 Chronicles 30:9)
- God is my help. **(Psalm 54:4)**
- God is merciful and forgiving.
  (Daniel 9:9)
- God is my rock, my salvation, my stronghold, my refuge, my Savior.
  (2 Samuel 22:3)
- God is mighty. **(Job 36:5)**
- God is a consuming fire.
  (Deuteronomy 4:24)
- God is a sun and shield. **(Psalm 84:11)**

Have each group discuss and present their answers to the class. **(15 minutes)**

Journal Writing

Have the students reflect and write in their journal:

1. Summarize what they have learned in this lesson.
2. How will this lesson impact their life? **(5 minutes)**

Closing prayer: We thank You God for the lessons we learned, our time of sharing and fellowship together. Now, help us to remember and apply these lessons to our daily lives. In the name of the Father, the Son and the Holy Spirit. Amen.

"...You are a part of the body of Christ.
God has chosen different ones in the church to do his work."
1 Corinthians 12:27-28

13

Personal Journal

And in him the whole building is joined together and rises to become a holy temple in the Lord. And in him you too are being built together to become a dwelling in which God lives by his Spirit. **(Ephesians 2:21-22)**

Take time to reflect and write about what you learned in this lesson as it relates to the Trinity and God Is.

Below are a few reminders from lesson 2 to assist with your personal journal writing:

- How would you describe the Trinity?
- God's love and ultimate desire is to be in relationship with humanity, to bring about redemption, wholeness and salvation.
- God's love permeates through time and space, from generation to generation.
- God's everlasting love will never lose its' power.

Prayer:
We open our hearts to you dear God to give us wisdom and understanding,
to guide us and teach us in knowledge and in truth. Amen.

*"...You are a part of the body of Christ.
God has chosen different ones in the church to do his work."*
1 Corinthians 12:27-28

Personal Journal:

Summarize what you have learned in this lesson.

_____

_____

_____

_____

_____

_____

_____

_____

_____

_____

How will this lesson impact your life?

_____

_____

_____

_____

_____

_____

_____

_____

_____

_____

_____

_____

"...You are a part of the body of Christ.
God has chosen different ones in the church to do his work."
1 Corinthians 12:27-28

15

LESSON III

JESUS CHRIST IS LORD

Lesson III—Jesus Christ is Lord

Opening Song: I am not forgotten

Prayer: Jesus Christ, give us the compassion, love, strength and power to become more like You. Let us live well and serve well in our Christian faith, both now and forever more. Amen.

Scripture: *But these are written that you may believe that Jesus is the Christ, the Son of God, and that by believing you may have life in his name.* **(John 20:31)**

Purpose:
- Jesus is the Son of God
- Jesus is the Christ
- Jesus is the Savior of the World

Material Needed:
- Easels, paper, pens, highlighters, magic markers
- NIV Youth Study Bibles
- Student Handout 9—Jesus Is
- Handout 9A—Jesus Is—Answer Sheet

Special Instructions: Students are encouraged to highlight scripture references in their Bible and keep a personal journal. For each group exercise, divide students into small groups of 5-7.

My Confirmation Goal

My Christian journey thus far has been one that was decided for me as a child. I am no longer a child. I am now at the age where I must decide if I want to accept God's free gift of salvation and make it my own.

My parents, guardians and church are here to help and guide me along this journey. However, the decision is now my responsibility. The instructions I receive during my confirmation classes will help me learn more about my faith.

While I am in the process of learning about my faith and how to be a Christian, I will not pretend to know all the answers. I am willing to learn all I can and to be all I can. I will give back to my church. I will live out my faith in my school, community and the world.

As a responsible youth, my confirmation will give me the opportunity to become an active member of the church body.

My profession of faith will allow the Holy Spirit to begin a new work in me and confirm me into the church. I affirm that my confirmation goal is to live out what my parents, guardians and church have accepted for me as an infant when I was baptized.

Jesus is the Son of God

Jesus Christ is the second part of the Godhead or the Trinity, God's gift of salvation.

- *For God so loved the world that he gave his One and Only Son, that whoever believes in him shall not perish but have eternal life.* **(John 3:16)**

Jesus as the Son of God means that He is both human and divine. He is God incarnated in the flesh. God took on himself in human nature (flesh) in order to reveal God (divinity) to people in a way that we could understand.

- *The Word became flesh and made his dwelling among us. We have seen his glory, the glory of the One and Only, who came from the Father, full of grace and truth.* **(John 1:14)**

"…You are a part of the body of Christ.
God has chosen different ones in the church to do his work."
1 Corinthians 12:27-28

19

Jesus is the Christ

The Bible tells us that the Israelites anxiously awaited a Messiah, who would come and destroy their enemies and establish once again their political position of power and authority in the world. As the Israelites waited for their Messiah, God sent an unlikely Savior in the form of a baby. He was born in a manger as a suffering servant, and not as a royal king. Christ as the Messiah, the anointed one of God, came not to establish an earthly kingdom, but to break the power of sin and death and to establish a heavenly kingdom.

Jesus is the Savior of the World

God sent his Son Jesus to save a world that was dying in sin.

God made him who had no sin to be sin for us, so that in him we might become the righteousness of God. **(2 Corinthians 5:21)**

Jesus came to bring reconciliation, to bring back together a world that had fallen away from God.

- Romans 5:11
- Romans 11:15
- 2 Corinthians 5:18-19/

Small Group Exercise I Part I

- Divide youth into small groups. Using their student Bibles, students will find and highlight the scriptures in the Gospel of John that describe the seven characteristics of Jesus:
  - John 6:35
  - John 8:12
  - John 10:9
  - John 10:11
  - John 11:25
  - John 14:6
  - John 15:1

Part II

- Have students complete Handout 9—Jesus Is.
  (10 minutes)
- **Answers:**
  Refer to Handout 9A—Jesus Is—Answer Sheet.
  (10 minutes)

Part III

- Using Handout 9A—Jesus Is, Answer Sheet, students are to draw a picture of each of these characteristics described by John. Students will need markers and easel paper to complete the project and present their answers to the class. **(30 minutes)**

Small Group Exercise II

Jesus is Savior

Divide students into small groups. Students are to find articles that best describe why we need Jesus as a Savior in our world today. Have students create a collage and a written response with their findings. Each group will need the following: markers, easel paper, old magazines, newspapers, tape or glue. Each group will present their project to the class. **(30 minutes)**

Journal Writing

Have the students reflect and write in their journal:

1. Summarize what they have learned in this lesson.
2. How will this lesson impact their life? **(5 minutes)**

Closing prayer: We thank You God for the lessons we learned and for our fellowship together. Now, help us remember and apply these lessons to our daily lives. In the name of the Father, the Son and the Holy Spirit. Amen.

20

"...You are a part of the body of Christ.
God has chosen different ones in the church to do his work."
1 Corinthians 12:27-28

Personal Journal

But these are written that you may believe that Jesus is the Christ, the Son of God, and that by believing you may have life in his name. **(John 20:30***)*

For God so loved the world that he gave his one and only Son, that whoever believes in him shall not perish but have eternal life. **(John 3:16)**

Take time to reflect and write about what you learned in this lesson as it relates to Jesus Christ is Lord.

Below are a few reminders from lesson 3 to assist with your personal journal writing:

- Jesus Christ is the second part of the Godhead or the Trinity.
- Jesus as the Son of God means that He is both human and divine.
- Jesus is God incarnated in the flesh. God took on himself in human nature (flesh) in order to reveal God (divinity) to people in a way that we could understand.
- Jesus is God's gift of salvation to the world.

Prayer:
Dear Lord, it is my desire to have compassion, love, strength, and power to become more like You. Help me to live well and serve well in my Christian faith. Amen.

*"...You are a part of the body of Christ.
God has chosen different ones in the church to do his work."*
1 Corinthians 12:27-28

21

Personal Journal:

Summarize what you have learned in this lesson.

_____

_____

_____

_____

_____

_____

_____

_____

_____

How will this lesson impact your life?

_____

_____

_____

_____

_____

_____

_____

_____

_____

_____

_____

*"...You are a part of the body of Christ.
God has chosen different ones in the church to do his work."*
1 Corinthians 12:27-28

LESSON IV

THE HOLY SPIRIT
OUR BAPTISM GIVEN
TO US BY GOD

Lesson IV—The Holy Spirit

Opening Song: I am not forgotten

Prayer: Come Holy Spirit with your quickening power. Warm our cold hearts. Help us to learn about Your power given to us from above. Amen.

Scripture: *Don't you know that you yourselves are God's temple and that God's Spirit lives in you?* **(1 Corinthians 3:16)**

Lesson Summary
*   What is the Holy Spirit
*   Life in the Spirit
*   Fruit of the Spirit

Material Needed:
*   Easels, paper, pens, highlighters
*   NIV Youth Study Bibles
*   Handout 10—The Holy Spirit Exercise I
*   Handout 10A—The Holy Spirit Exercise I Answer Sheet
*   Handout 11—Fruit of the Spirit
*   Magic markers

Special Instructions: Students are encouraged to highlight Bible scripture references and to keep a personal journal. Students should be divided into small groups of 5-7.

My Confirmation Goal

My Christian journey thus far has been one that was decided for me when I was a child. I am no longer a child. I am now at the age where I must decide if I want to accept God's free gift of salvation and make it my own.

My parents, guardians and church are here to help and guide me along this journey. However, the decision is now my responsibility. The instructions I receive during my confirmation classes will help me learn more about my faith.

While I am in the process of learning about my faith and how to be a Christian, I will not pretend to know all the answers. I am willing to learn all I can and to be all I can. I will give

back to my church. I will live out my faith in my school, community and the world. As a responsible youth, my confirmation will give me the opportunity to become an active member of the church body.

My profession of faith will allow the Holy Spirit to begin a new work in me and confirm me into the church. I affirm that my confirmation goal is to live out what my parents, guardians and church have accepted for me as an infant when I was baptized.

What is the Holy Spirit?

The Holy Spirit is the third part of the Godhead or the Trinity.
*   *It is the life-giving Spirit that was actively present with God in the creation of the world.* **(see Genesis 1:2)**
*   *The Holy Spirit is our comforter and counselor to help guide us in holiness, and righteousness and in all things in life.* **(see John 14:16)**

The Holy Spirit is our teacher
*   *The Holy Spirit was sent by God to teach and bring back to our remembrance all that is written in the Word of God.* **(see John 14:26)**
*   *The Holy Spirit is the Spirit of truth.* **(see John 15:26)**

The Holy Spirit is our baptism given to us by God:

*   Isaiah 44:3
*   Joel 2:28-29
*   Zechariah 12:10
*   Matthew 3:11
*   Matthew 3:16
*   Mark 1:8

"...You are a part of the body of Christ.
God has chosen different ones in the church to do his work."
1 Corinthians 12:27-28

25

The Holy Spirit lives in us:

- Romans 8:9
- 1 Corinthians 3:16
- 2 Corinthians 13:14

Exercise I

Divide the students into small groups.

Using their student Bible, and Handout 10—The Holy Spirit, have each group fill out the handout and also highlight in their Bibles the scriptures listed below:

- 1 Corinthians 12:13
- Ephesians 4:30
- Romans 8:16
- Titus 3:5
- John 16:13
- Romans 8:14
- Ephesians 5:18
- Romans 8:26

See Handout 10A—Holy Spirit—Answer Sheet. **(15 minutes)**

Life in the Spirit

On the day of Pentecost **(see Act 2:1-4)** the Holy Spirit was manifested in the lives of the believers of Jesus Christ. This out pouring of the Spirit gave power to the believer to live their life free without condemnation. **(see Romans 8:1)**

Through the power of the Spirit leading and guiding our lives, we become more like Christ. As believers, our new life in Christ is the beginning of our Christian experience. The doors are now opened for us to be adopted into the family of God. We are now God's heirs and co-heirs with Christ.

- Romans 8:14-17
- Galatians 4:6-7

Without the Spirit of Christ living in us **(see Romans 8:9)**, we cannot become Christians. The Spirit unites every believer into a Christian community. We are one in the body of Christ; there are no strangers, we are citizens of God's kingdom.

- Ephesians 2:19-22
- 1 Corinthians 12:11
- Ephesians 4:4

Fruit of the Spirit

The Fruit of the Spirit are nine biblical characteristics produced within us by the Holy Spirit. These characteristics identifies a believer's life in Jesus Christ:

- *Love, joy, peace, patience, kindness, goodness, faithfulness, gentleness and self-control.* **(Galatians 5:22-23)**

These characteristics are not individual fruit working independently of one another, but collectively working together in us signifying that we are representing the body of Christ. (Have students read Handout 11—Fruit of the Spirit)

Exercise II

Each group is to develop a skit based upon the scenario below. The objective of the skit is to use the nine fruit of the Spirit to win a person to Christ.

Scenario for Exercise II

A young person whom every member of the group knows is hanging out with the wrong crowd. This person has shown symptoms of depression possibly from drugs and poor self-esteem. If nothing is done to help the person, they may commit suicide. **(30 minutes)**

Upon completion of the skit, each group will present their skit to the class.

Journal Writing

Have the students reflect and write in their journal:
1. Summarize what they have learned in this lesson.
2. How will this lesson impact their life? **(5 minutes)**

"...You are a part of the body of Christ.
God has chosen different ones in the church to do his work."
1 Corinthians 12:27-28

Closing prayer: We thank You God for the lesson we learned and for our fellowship together. Now, help us remember and apply these lessons to our daily lives. In the name of the Father, the Son and the Holy Spirit. Amen.

Personal Journal

Don't you know that you yourselves are God's temple and that God's Spirit lives in you?
(1 Corinthians 3:16)

**Take time to reflect and write about what you learned in
this lesson as it relates to the Holy Spirit.**

Below are a few reminders from lesson 4 to assist with your personal journal writing:

- The Holy Spirit serves a very import part of who I am in Christ.
- As a believer my new life in Christ is the beginning of my Christian experience.
- I am now adopted into the family of God as a co-heir with Christ through the anointing of the Holy Spirit.
- The nine Fruit of the Spirit are valuable in my life as a Christian.

Prayer:
Come Holy Spirit with your quickening power and warm my heart.
Help me to learn more about the gift of the Spirit. Amen.

*"...You are a part of the body of Christ.
God has chosen different ones in the church to do his work."*
1 Corinthians 12:27-28

27

Personal Journal:

Summarize what you have learned in this lesson.

_____

_____

_____

_____

_____

_____

_____

_____

_____

How will this lesson impact your life?

_____

_____

_____

_____

_____

_____

_____

_____

_____

_____

_____

"...You are a part of the body of Christ.
God has chosen different ones in the church to do his work."
1 Corinthians 12:27-28

LESSON V

SALVATION SET
APART BY GOD

Lesson V—Salvation

Opening Song: I am not forgotten

Prayer: Heavenly Father, use me for Your glory. This day I am open and ready to give You my life. I desire to become the person You created me to be. This is my prayer in the name of Jesus the Christ. Amen

Scripture: *Brothers and sisters, I do not consider myself yet to have taken hold of it. But one thing I do: Forgetting what is behind and straining toward what is ahead, I press on toward the goal to win the prize for which God has called me heavenward in Christ Jesus.* **(Philippians 3:13-14)**

Lesson Summary
- What is Salvation

Material Needed:
- Easels, paper, pen, highlighters, magic markers
- NIV Youth Study Bibles

Special Instructions: Students are encouraged to highlight scripture references in their Bibles and keep a personal journal. For each group exercise, divide students into small groups of 5-7.

My Confirmation Goal

My Christian journey thus far has been one that was decided for me when I was a child. I am no longer a child. I am now at the age where I must decide if I want to accept God's free gift of salvation and make it my own.

My parents, guardians and church are here to help and guide me along this journey. However, the decision is now my responsibility. The instructions I receive during my confirmation classes will help me learn more about my faith.

While I am in the process of learning about my faith and how to be a Christian, I will not pretend to know all the answers. I am willing to learn all I can and to be all I can. I will give back to my church. I will live out my faith in my school, community and the world.

As a responsible youth, my confirmation will give me the opportunity to become an active member of the church body.

My profession of faith will allow the Holy Spirit to begin a new work in me and confirm me into the church. I affirm that my confirmation goal is to live out what my parents, guardians and church have accepted for me as an infant when I was baptized.

What Is Salvation?

Salvation means that you have been sanctified or set apart by God with a new life.

Salvation is an act of confessing

A person must confess with their mouth and believe in their heart that Jesus is Lord. Once a person confesses and accepts Jesus Christ as Lord, all of their sins are forgiven. After this act of confession is made, no matter who you are, where you are, or what wrongs are committed, by the grace of God you will be saved. **(see Romans 10:9-10)**

- *The wages of sin which is death (but now you) have the gift of God which is eternal life in Christ Jesus our Lord.* **(Romans 6:23)**

Salvation is a free gift

We were created to live and to spend an eternity with God. Sin separated us from God's divine plan of eternal life. In order to renew our relationship, God devised a way to remove sin. This is called God's plan of salvation.

"...You are a part of the body of Christ.
God has chosen different ones in the church to do his work."
1 Corinthians 12:27-28

31

Salvation is not earned by good deeds or purchased with money. It is a gift from God. **(see Ephesians 2:8-9)** The price of salvation was purchased long ago with the precious blood of Jesus Christ, when He died on the Cross.

- Salvation is a free gift given to all who believe in Jesus Christ.
- Salvation is found in no one else, for there is no other name under heaven given to men by which we must be saved. **(Acts 4:12)**
- Salvation reunites us to God our Creator.

Salvation is personal

Your confession and acceptance of Jesus Christ as a youth has created a special relationship. Now, Jesus is your personal Savior. He has cleansed your life from sin and guaranteed you with the promise of eternal life.

- John 3:16
- John 3:36

Exercise I

This exercise is designed to give students biblical references that will help youth with their understanding of salvation. **(20 minutes)**

Using the assigned scriptures listed below, each group will find and write their answers to the following questions. Answers for students are provided below and in Handout 12—Salvation Answer Sheet.

What is the promise given? (John 6:37)

- *Whoever comes to me, I will never drive away.*

What are the four promises? (John 10:28-29)

- *I give them eternal life, and they shall never perish.*
- *No one will snatch them out of my hand*
- *My Father, who has given them to me, is greater than all.*
- *No one can snatch them out of my Father's hand.*

What are the two factors that confirm your salvation? (Ephesians 2:8)

- *Grace—Faith*

What are two ways you can earn salvation? (Ephesians 2:9)

- *Nothing—It is a gift*

What are the ten reasons listed that confirm your salvation? (Romans 8:38-39)

- ***Death***—*you cannot lose your salvation through death.*
- ***Life***—*you cannot lose your salvation while you are alive.*
- ***Angels***—*have no power over your salvation.*
- ***Demons***—*cannot take your salvation away.*
- ***The present***—*nothing in this present life can take your salvation from you.*
- ***The future***—*no matter what happens in the future your salvation will not change.*
- ***Any powers***—*there are no powers strong enough to remove your salvation.*
- ***Height***—*there is nothing above you that can prevent your salvation.*
- ***Depth***—*there is nothing below you that can get beneath your salvation.*
- ***Nor anything else***—*nothing in all creation shall be able to separate us from the love of God, that is in Christ Jesus our Lord.*

Exercise II

Each group will use the findings in Exercise I to convince a new believer that they are saved and their salvation is secure. Each small group will share their answers with the entire group. **(20 minutes)**

Journal Writing

Have the students reflect and write in their journal:

1. Summarize what they have learned in this lesson.
2. How will this lesson impact their life? **(5 minutes)**

Closing Prayer: I thank You God for my free gift of salvation. Now that I am saved, I recognize that all things have passed away. My old habits and thoughts are in my past. I am now a new creation in Christ Jesus with the promise of eternal life. Because of my free gift and what it means to me, I will diligently strive to live out my faith. Amen.

*"...You are a part of the body of Christ.
God has chosen different ones in the church to do his work."*
1 Corinthians 12:27-28

Personal Journal

. . . Forgetting what is behind and straining toward what is ahead, I press on toward the goal to win the prize for which God has called me heavenward in Christ Jesus. **(Philippians 3:13-14)**

**Take time to reflect and write about what you learned
in this lesson as it relates to Salvation.**

Below are a few reminders from lesson 5 to assist with your personal journal writing.

- Salvation means I have been sanctified or set apart by God with a new life.
- When God created me I was created to live and not die but to spend an eternity with God.
- My sin separated me from God's divine plan. In order to renew my relationship, God devised a way to remove my sin. This is called God's plan of salvation.

Prayer:
I thank you God for my free gift of salvation. Now that I am saved, I recognize
that all things have passed away, including my old habits and thoughts. I am now
a new creation in Christ Jesus with the promise of eternal life. Amen

*"...You are a part of the body of Christ.
God has chosen different ones in the church to do his work."*
1 Corinthians 12:27-28

33

Summarize what you have learned in this lesson.

_____

_____

_____

_____

_____

_____

_____

_____

_____

_____

How will this lesson impact your life?

_____

_____

_____

_____

_____

_____

_____

_____

_____

_____

_____

_____

"...You are a part of the body of Christ.
God has chosen different ones in the church to do his work."
1 Corinthians 12:27-28

LESSON VI

HOW WE WORSHIP-
WHERE WE WORSHIP-
THE WAY WE WORSHIP

Lesson VI—Worship

Opening Song: I am not forgotten

Prayer: We open our hearts to You dear God. Give us wisdom and understanding to guide and teach us in knowledge and in truth. Create within us a desire to learn your purpose for our lives. Help us to grow in our faith. Amen.

Scripture: *Worship the LORD with gladness; come before him with joyful songs.* **(Psalm 100:2)**

Lesson Summary

- Defining Worship
- Where We Worship
- The Way We Worship
- How We Worship
- Worship Terms and Definitions

Material Needed:

- Easels, paper, pens, highlighters, magic markers
- NIV Youth Study Bibles

Special Instructions: Students are encouraged to highlight scripture references in their Bibles and keep a personal journal. For each group exercise, divide students into small groups of 5-7.

My Confirmation Goal

My Christian journey thus far has been one that was decided for me when I was a child. I am no longer a child. I am now at the age where I must decide if I want to accept God's free gift of salvation and make it my own.

My parents, guardians and my church are here to help and guide me along this journey. However, the decision is now my responsibility. The instructions I receive during my confirmation classes will help me to learn more about my faith.

While I am in the process of learning about my faith and how to be a Christian, I will not pretend to know all the answers. I am willing to learn all I can and to be all I can. I will give back to my church. I will live out my faith in my school, community and the world.

As a responsible youth, my confirmation will give me the opportunity to become an active member of the church body.

My profession of faith will allow the Holy Spirit to begin a new work in me and confirm me into the church. I affirm that my confirmation goal is to live out what my parents, guardians and church have accepted for me as an infant when I was baptized.

Defining Worship

Worship can be a private or public activity. Worship can be an individual experience or whenever a specific community of people gather together.

Where We Worship

The activity of worship is generally at a specific time and place. For Christians, this is normally in churches within a local community.

The Way We Worship

We worship with symbols, rituals, people speaking, singing, dancing, music, prayers and in silence.

How We Worship

The four acts of worship are:

- Praise
- Adoration
- Thanksgiving
- Petition

"...You are a part of the body of Christ. God has chosen different ones in the church to do his work."
1 Corinthians 12:27-28

37

Praise is giving honor and adoration to God as a celebration of God's being and worth.

- *Praise the Lord. Give thanks to the Lord, for he is good; his love endures forever.* **(Psalm 106:1)**
- *Praise the Lord, all you nations; extol him, all you peoples. For great is his love toward us, and the faithfulness of the Lord endures forever. Praise the Lord.* **(Psalm 117)**
- *Praise the name of the Lord; praise him, you servants of the Lord.* **(Psalm 135:1)**
- *How good it is to sing praises to our God, how pleasant and fitting to praise him!* **(Psalm 147:1)**
  Praise the LORD. Praise God in his sanctuary; praise him in his mighty heavens. Praise him for his acts of power; praise him for his surpassing greatness. Praise him with the sounding of the trumpet, praise him with the harp and lyre, praise him with tambourine and dancing, praise him with the strings and flute, praise him with the clash of cymbals, praise him with resounding cymbals. Let everything that has breath praise the LORD. Praise the LORD! **(Psalm 150)**

Adoration is the true worship of recognizing God alone as our ultimate Lord.

Thanksgiving is our expression of gratitude. It is a type of prayer in which believers offer their gratitude to God for all the blessings and goodness received.

Petition is a portion of a prayer that is composed of supplications or requests. We can also make petitions for others through intercessions.

- *I prayed for this child, and the Lord has granted me what I asked of him.* **(1 Samuel 1:27)**

- *May we shout for joy over your victory and lift up our banners in the name of our God. May the Lord grant all your requests.* **(Psalm 20:5)**
- *Do not be anxious about anything, but in every situation, by prayer and petition, with thanksgiving, present your requests to God.* **(Philippians 4:6)**
- *And pray in the Spirit on all occasions with all kinds of prayers and requests. With this in mind, be alert and always keep on praying for all the Lord's people.* **(Ephesians 6:18)**

Exercise I

In their groups, youth are to identify the way they worship God in their church, community and daily lives. Each group should write on easel paper the various ways they worship. Each small group will share their answers with the entire group. **(20 minutes)**

Exercise II

This is a two-part exercise; divide groups into two sections.

Exercise for Group I—youth are to spend time identifying the symbols of their Christian faith such as the cross, bread, wine, the pulpit, kneeling rail etc. The group will need newspapers, magazines, cut-outs and individual drawings to complete their project. Youth are to place their findings (symbols) on easel paper.

Exercise for Group 2—youth are to spend time identifying the various rituals such as prayer, preaching, communion and baptism used in a worship setting. This group will also need newspapers, magazines, cut-outs and individual drawings to complete their project. Youth are to place their findings (rituals) on easel paper.

"...You are a part of the body of Christ. God has chosen different ones in the church to do his work."
1 Corinthians 12:27-28

After each group completes their exercise they will present their final project. **(30 minutes)**

Exercise III

In their small groups they will be assigned one of the four forms of worship.

- Praise
- Adoration
- Thanksgiving
- Petition

The separate groups are to develop a prayer on easel paper with an emphasis on the form of worship assigned to their group. While the main focus must be on their assigned form of worship, each group should also include the other three forms of worship in their prayer.

At the conclusion of this assignment have each group present their prayers to the class. **(30 minutes)**

Journal Writing

Have the students reflect and write in their journal:

1. Summarize what they have learned in this lesson.
2. How will this lesson impact their life? **(5 minutes)**

Closing Prayer: I thank You God for my worship experience. I adore You. I will praise and exalt Your name forever in my worship and life. Amen.

"...You are a part of the body of Christ.
God has chosen different ones in the church to do his work."
1 Corinthians 12:27-28

39

WORSHIP TERMS AND DEFINITIONS

The Liturgy
- The various acts of worship offered to God by the people are called a Liturgy.
- The worship service is a time and place where people come together and show their love for God, through songs, prayers, praise, dance and proclamation of the gospel.

WORSHIP TERMS AND DEFINITIONS

The Prelude
The Lord is in His Holy temple, Let all the earth keep silence before Him.
(Habakkuk 2:20)

- "Worship begins when you enter the sanctuary."
- Prelude is the music that is played at the very beginning of the worship service.[iv] This allows a person to enter into a sacred space and place to reflect and engage in silent prayer to God.

- The prelude is to remind and reinforce that we are on "Holy Ground" and should conduct ourselves accordingly.

"...You are a part of the body of Christ.
God has chosen different ones in the church to do his work."
1 Corinthians 12:27-28

WORSHIP TERMS AND DEFINITIONS

Hymns

Speak to one another with psalms, hymns and spiritual songs. Sing and make music in your heart to the Lord. **(Ephesians 5:19)**

- Hymns are songs of praise, prayer and thanksgiving sung at different times in the worship service.
- Hymns help us to praise God. They provide an almost mystical connection with the endless anthems of praise. They unite the Lord's earth-bound church in heavenly harmony. (My Faith Looks Up to Thee—We Praise Thee, O God)
- Hymns enable us to pray when we can't find the right words to say. (Father, I Stretch My Hands to Thee—Guide Me, O Thou Great Jehovah)
- Hymns give us a way of talking to ourselves or encouraging ourselves in the Lord. (Blessed Assurance, Jesus is Mine—Be Still My Soul—The Lord Is On My Side)
- Hymns connect us with past generations of believers who composed songs that were sung by Christians from every era and branch of Christendom[v]

*"...You are a part of the body of Christ.
God has chosen different ones in the church to do his work."*
1 Corinthians 12:27-28

41

WORSHIP TERMS AND DEFINITIONS

The Invocation
When Solomon finished praying, fire came down from heaven and consumed the burnt offering and the sacrifices, and the glory of the Lord filled the temple. **(2 Chronicles 7:1)**

• The invocation is a prayer petition or an appeal to God calling for the presence of the Holy Spirit to be a part of the worship service.
• The invocation is usually at the beginning of the worship service.

WORSHIP TERMS AND DEFINITIONS

The Scripture Reading
The scroll of the prophet Isaiah was handed to him. Unrolling it, he found the place where it is written. The spirit of the Lord is on me, because he has anointed me to preach good news to the poor. He has sent me to proclaim freedom for the prisoners and recovery of sight for the blind, to release the oppressed, to proclaim the year of the Lord's favor. Then he rolled up the scroll, gave it back to the attendant and sat down. **(Luke 4:17-20)**

• A scripture is generally selected from the Old Testament, one of the four gospels (Matthew, Mark, Luke or John) and from one of the New Testament Epistles.
• The scripture readings are determined by a liturgical calendar. (A liturgical calendar is a Christian calendar of events i.e., Advent, Epiphany, the Lenten season, Easter and Pentecost).

"...You are a part of the body of Christ.
God has chosen different ones in the church to do his work."
1 Corinthians 12:27-28

WORSHIP TERMS AND DEFINITIONS

The Sermonic Hymn
Sing to the Lord a new song; sing to the Lord, all the earth. Sing to the Lord, praise his name; proclaim his salvation day after day. **(Psalm 96:1-2)**

•   A song of preparation sung before the sermon, the sermonic hymn sets the tone for the preaching moment or the proclamation of the gospel.

WORSHIP TERMS AND DEFINITIONS

The Sermon or the Preached Word
How, then, can they call the one they have not believed in? And how can they believe in the one of whom they have not heard? And how can they hear without someone preaching to them? **(Romans 10:14)**

•   The preached word is the center of our worship experience.
•   The preached word is called a Sermon.
•   The preached word is based on the Holy Scriptures.

"…You are a part of the body of Christ.
God has chosen different ones in the church to do his work."
1 Corinthians 12:27-28

43

WORSHIP TERMS AND DEFINITIONS

The Invitation to Christian Discipleship
> *Peter replied, "Repent and be baptized, every one of you, in the*
> *name of Jesus Christ for the forgiveness of your sins.*
> **(Acts 2:38)**

- The Invitation to Christian Discipleship is inviting others to give their life to Christ and to receive salvation.
- It can also be a time for special prayer requests and rededication of one's life to Christ.

WORSHIP TERMS AND DEFINITIONS

Offerings
> *The Lord said to Moses, Tell the Israelites to bring me and offering.*
> *You are to receive the offering for me for each man whose*
> *heart prompts him to give.* **(Exodus 25:1)**

- An opportunity to worship the Lord in our giving is called an offering.
- Benevolent offerings or missionary offerings are used to support the poor, needy, and other ministries of the church.
- General offerings support the overall work of the church.
- A tithe is a tenth of what you have earned and what is requested of God.

"…You are a part of the body of Christ.
God has chosen different ones in the church to do his work."
1 Corinthians 12:27-28

WORSHIP TERMS AND DEFINITIONS

The Doxology

"Praise God from whom all blessings flow; Praise Him all creatures here below; Praise Him above ye heavenly host; Praise Father, Son and Holy Ghost, Amen.[vi]

- Traditional worship service is often opened and closed with a short hymn of praise sung by the choir and congregation.
- The Doxology recognizes that we are in God's house and in the presence of the Lord.

To him who is able to keep you from falling and to present you before his glorious presence without fault and with great joy to the only god our Savior be glory, majesty, power and authority, through Jesus Christ our Lord, before all ages, now and forevermore! Amen.
(Jude 1:24-25)

WORSHIP TERMS AND DEFINITIONS

The Benediction

May the grace of the Lord Jesus Christ, and the love of God, and the fellowship of the Holy Spirit be with you all. **(2 Corinthians 13:14)**

- The benediction is a final prayer asking God's blessings and protection over our lives as we leave the worship service.
- Benedictions are recorded in both the Old and New Testament Scriptures. Some examples are: Numbers 6:24-26; Psalm 121:7-8; and Jude 1:24-25.

"...You are a part of the body of Christ.
God has chosen different ones in the church to do his work."
1 Corinthians 12:27-28

45

Personal Journal

Worship the LORD with gladness; come before him with joyful songs. **(Psalm 100:2)**

**Take time to reflect and write about what you learned
in this lesson as it relates to Worship.**

Below are a few reminders from lesson 6 to assist with your personal journal writing:

- The activity of worship is generally at a specific time and place.
- Worship involves the use of symbols, rituals, people speaking, singing, dancing music, prayers, and even silence within our faith community.

Prayer:
I worship you God! I will continuously praise and exalt your
name forever in all forms of worship. Amen.

*"...You are a part of the body of Christ.
God has chosen different ones in the church to do his work."*
1 Corinthians 12:27-28

Personal Journal:

Summarize what you have learned in this lesson.

_____

_____

_____

_____

_____

_____

_____

_____

_____

_____

How will this lesson impact your life?

_____

_____

_____

_____

_____

_____

_____

_____

_____

_____

_____

_____

"...You are a part of the body of Christ.
God has chosen different ones in the church to do his work."
1 Corinthians 12:27-28

47

LESSON VII

THE BIBLE-WHAT I BELIEVE-
GENERAL CONFESSION

Lesson VII

The Bible, What I Believe, General Confession

Opening Song: I am not forgotten

Prayer: We open our hearts to You dear God. Give us wisdom and understanding to guide and teach us in knowledge and in truth. Create within us a desire to learn Your purpose for our lives. Help us to grow in our faith. Amen.

Scripture: *All Scripture is God-breathed and is useful for teaching, rebuking, correcting and training in righteousness, so that the servant of God may be thoroughly equipped for every good work.* **(2 Timothy 3:16-17)**

Lesson Summary

- The Bible
- The Books of the Old Testament
- The Books of the New Testament
- What I Believe
- The General Confession

Principle teaching: To help youth understand the value and meaning of certain tenets of their Christian faith and church.

Material Needed:

- Paper, pens, highlighters, magic markers
- Prizes (prizes should be awarded to student(s) and their groups to challenge and encourage them to memorize the material in each of the four exercises.)
- NIV Youth Study Bibles

Special Instructions:

Encourage students to review the books of the Bible with you. This will help youth to become familiar with where the books are located.

My Confirmation Goal

My Christian journey thus far has been one that was decided for me when I was a child. I am no longer a child. I am now at the age where I must decide if I want to accept God's free gift of salvation and make it my own.

My parents, guardians and church are here to help and guide me along this journey. However, the decision is now my responsibility. The instructions I receive during my confirmation classes will help me learn more about my faith.

While I am in the process of learning about my faith and how to be a Christian, I will not pretend to know all the answers. I am willing to learn all I can and to be all I can. I will give back to my church. I will live out my faith in my school, community and the world.

As a responsible youth, my confirmation will give me the opportunity to become an active member of the church body.

My profession of faith will allow the Holy Spirit to begin a new work in me and confirm me into the church.

I affirm that my confirmation goal is to live out what my parents, guardians and church have accepted for me as an infant when I was baptized.

"...You are a part of the body of Christ.
God has chosen different ones in the church to do his work."
1 Corinthians 12:27-28

51

Exercise I

After a review of the **Old Testament**, divide students into small groups. Give each group time to memorize:

- The 5 books of laws
- The 12 books of history
- The 5 books of poetry
- The 17 books of prophecy

Students should use the table of contents in their NIV Study Bibles for their reference.

Each group must determine among themselves who will memorize the 5 books of laws; 12 books of history; 5 books of poetry; and the 17 books of prophecy. **(20 minutes)**

Following the above mentioned exercise, each group will present what they have memorized.

Exercise II

After review of the **New Testament**, each group is to memorize:

- The 4 Books of the Gospel
- The 1 Book of History
- The 21 Letters
- The 1 Book of Prophecy

Students should use the table of contents in their NIV Study Bibles for their reference.

Each group must determine among themselves who will memorize the 4 books of the Gospel; the 1 book of history; the 21 letters; and the 1 book of prophecy.
(20 minutes)

Following the above mentioned exercise, each group will present what they have memorized.

Exercise III

After reviewing What I Believe, students are to *memorize* and write down each of them.
(20 minutes)

Review each of What I Believe and have the class *recite* them as a class.

Exercise IV

After reviewing the General Confession with the students, have the students write down and *memorize* the principle components.
(20 minutes)

Review the principle components and have the class *recite* the General Confession.

Exercise Presentation:

Each group will be given time after each exercise to present what they have learned and memorized. Prizes will be awarded to student(s) and groups with the best presentation and memory accuracy at the end of each exercise.

Journal Writing

Have the students reflect and write in their journal:

1. Summarize what they have learned in this lesson.
2. How will this lesson impact their life?
   (5 minutes)

Closing Prayer: We thank You God for the lesson we learned, and for our fellowship together. Now, help us remember and apply these lessons to our daily lives. In the name of the Father, the Son and the Holy Spirit. Amen.

"...You are a part of the body of Christ.
God has chosen different ones in the church to do his work."
1 Corinthians 12:27-28

THE BIBLE

*I am the Alpha and the Omega, says the Lord God, who is, and who
was, and who is to come, the Almighty.* **(Revelation 1:8)**

What is the Bible?

- The Bible is the inspiring Word of God, a spiritual book consisting of God's laws, commandments and promises for the people of God. Through history, poetry, prophecy and letters we learn about God, what God is like, what God has done and what God desires for humankind.
- The Bible foretells of the coming of the Messiah, Christ Jesus our Lord, His life, birth, death, resurrection and God's plan of salvation.

THE BIBLE

What is the Bible?

- The Bible describes how God created the world and how sin came into the world separating humankind from God. **(See Genesis 3:14-19)**
- The Bible is about God's love and His Son Jesus Christ who came to restore humankind back to God through the forgiveness of sins.

*For God did not send his Son into the world to condemn the world,
but to save the world through him.* **(John 3:17)**

*"...You are a part of the body of Christ.
God has chosen different ones in the church to do his work."*
1 Corinthians 12:27-28

53

THE BIBLE

Who wrote the Bible?

- The writers of the Bible were ordinary people just like you and I. They were chosen by God to write the present and future biblical record of events during their time and the time to come. The stories were later compiled and printed by biblical scholars.

BOOKS OF THE OLD TESTAMENT

- These Five books are called the "Torah" or the books of laws:
    Genesis—Exodus—Leviticus—Numbers—Deuteronomy

- The Five Books Cover:
    - The **Creation** of the world
    - The **Beginning** of the nation of Israel
    - The **Exodus** of God's chosen people out of Egypt
    - The **Laws** that governed God's chosen People

"...You are a part of the body of Christ.
God has chosen different ones in the church to do his work."
1 Corinthians 12:27-28

BOOKS OF THE OLD TESTAMENT

History

- The historical events of Jewish history consist of twelve books of the Bible:
  Joshua—Judges—Ruth—1 Samuel—2 Samuel—1 Kings—2 Kings
  1 Chronicles—2 Chronicles—Ezra—Nehemiah—Esther

- The Books Cover:
  - The period when the children of Israel entered into the promise land.
  - The period of Judges, Kings, the captivity of the Israelites and their return to Jerusalem.

BOOKS OF THE OLD TESTAMENT

Poetry

- There are five books of poetry in the Bible:
  Job—Psalm—Proverbs—Ecclesiastes—Song of Solomon

- The Hebrew writers used poetry to express many feelings: from sadness to happiness, from fear to praise, to God's protection and love.

"...You are a part of the body of Christ.
God has chosen different ones in the church to do his work."
1 Corinthians 12:27-28

55

BOOKS OF THE OLD TESTAMENT

Prophecy

- God spoke to Israel through seventeen different prophets.
- The first five prophets are called "major" prophets. Their books are much longer than the last twelve books of prophets called "minor" prophets.
- Throughout the Old Testament the children of Israel often received messages direct from God through these prophets.

BOOKS OF THE OLD TESTAMENT

The Five Major Prophets:

Isaiah—Jeremiah—Lamentations—Ezekiel—Daniel

"…You are a part of the body of Christ.
God has chosen different ones in the church to do his work."
1 Corinthians 12:27-28

BOOKS OF THE OLD TESTAMENT

The Twelve Minor Prophets:

Hosea—Joel—Amos—Obadiah—Jonah—Micah—Nahum—
Habakkuk Zephaniah—Haggai—Zechariah—Malachi

BOOKS OF THE OLD TESTAMENT

Laws	**5** Books
History	**12** Books
Poetry	**5** Books
Prophecy	**17** Books
	39 Books

"...You are a part of the body of Christ.
God has chosen different ones in the church to do his work."
1 Corinthians 12:27-28

57

BOOKS OF THE NEW TESTAMENT

The Gospels:

*   The first four books of the New Testament are called the Gospels.
    Matthew—Mark—Luke—John

*   These books tell the story of Jesus, His birth, miracles, teachings, death and resurrection.

BOOKS OF THE NEW TESTAMENT

The Book of "Acts"

*   This is the only history book in the New Testament.
*   In the book of Acts we learn how the church began and the many persecutions of Christians.

*"...You are a part of the body of Christ.
God has chosen different ones in the church to do his work."*
1 Corinthians 12:27-28

BOOKS OF THE NEW TESTAMENT

- There are twenty-one letters or epistles written to individuals and the early church:
  Romans—1 Corinthians—2 Corinthians—Galatians—Ephesians
  Philippians—Colossians—1 Thessalonians—2 Thessalonians

  1 Timothy—2 Timothy—Titus—Philemon—Hebrews—James
  1 Peter—2 Peter—1 John—2 John—3 John—Jude

- These letters were written to correct some of the problems in the early church. They were also written to give instructions on how to live a Christian life.

BOOKS OF THE NEW TESTAMENT

The Book of "Revelation"

- This is the only New Testament book of prophecy.
- The book of Revelation gives us an account of a vision given to the Apostle John by God about:
  - The problems of the seven churches **(See Revelation 2:1-3:22)**
  - The end time prophecy **(See Revelation 13)**
  - The establishment of a new heaven and earth **(See Revelation 21:1-27)**
  - The return of Christ **(See Revelations 22:7-16)**

*"...You are a part of the body of Christ.
God has chosen different ones in the church to do his work."*
1 Corinthians 12:27-28

59

BOOKS OF THE NEW TESTAMENT

The Gospels	**4** Books
History	**1** Book
Letters	**21** Books
Prophecy	**1** Book
	27 Books

WHAT I BELIEVE

1. I believe in God the Father Almighty, maker of heaven and earth.
   - **(Ephesians 4:6)**
2. I believe in Jesus Christ, His only Son, our Lord.
   - **(John 1:14; 3:16-18)**
3. I believe He was conceived by the Holy Spirit
   - **(Luke 1:35; Matthew 1:18-20)**
4. I believe He was born of the Virgin Mary
   - **(Isaiah 7:14; Matthew 1:20-25)**
5. I believe He suffered under Pontius Pilate
   - **(Mark 15:15)**

"...You are a part of the body of Christ.
God has chosen different ones in the church to do his work."
1 Corinthians 12:27-28

REW
MINISTRIES

WHAT I BELIEVE

6.   I believe He was crucified dead and buried.
     o   **(1 Corinthians 15:4; Acts 2:20-37)**
7.   I believe He arose on the third day from the dead.
     o   **(1 Corinthians 15:4; Acts 10:40)**
8.   I believe in the Holy Spirit.
     o   **(John 14:26; John 15:26; Acts 1:8; Acts 2:3-4)**
9.   I believe in the Church Universal.
     o   **(Romans 12:5; 1 Corinthians 10:17)**
10. I believe in the communion of saints.
     o   **(Acts 2:42-47; 1 Corinthians 10:16-17)**

WHAT I BELIEVE

11. I believe in the forgiveness of sin.
     o   **(Luke 24:47; Col 1:14; 1 Peter 1:18-19)**
12. I believe in the resurrection of the body.
     o   **(Revelations 20:12-13; 1 Corinthians 15:13-23)**
13. I believe in life everlasting
     o   **(Matthew 25:46; John 3:15-16)**

"...You are a part of the body of Christ.
God has chosen different ones in the church to do his work."
1 Corinthians 12:27-28

61

GENERAL CONFESSION

"Come now, and let us reason together,"
Says the Lord," Though your sins are like scarlet,
They shall be as white as snow; Though they are red like crimson, They shall be as wool.
(Isaiah 1:18)

A Confession is:
- A humble admission of a person's wrongful thoughts, words, and deeds.
- We acknowledgement our sins and shortcomings before Almighty God and seek forgiveness through Christ Jesus our Lord

GENERAL CONFESSION

- Almighty God, Father of our Lord Jesus Christ, Maker of all things, Judge of all people, we acknowledge and bewail our manifold sins and wickedness which we from time to time most grievously have committed by thought, word, and deed against Your Divine Majesty, provoking most justly your wrath and indignation against us. We do earnestly repent and are heartily sorry for these our misdoings; the remembrance of them is grievous unto us.
- Have mercy upon us, have mercy upon us, most merciful Father for Your Son our Lord Jesus Christ's sake; forgive us all that is past, and grant that we may ever hereafter serve and please You in newness of life, to the honor and glory of Your name, through Jesus Christ our Lord, Amen.[vii]

"...You are a part of the body of Christ.
God has chosen different ones in the church to do his work."
1 Corinthians 12:27-28

PRINCIPLE COMPONENTS OF A CONFESSION

1. **We acknowledge** or confess our sins.
   We ask God:
2. For mercy
3. For forgiveness
5. For newness of life
6. Through Jesus Christ our Lord

"...You are a part of the body of Christ.
God has chosen different ones in the church to do his work."
1 Corinthians 12:27-28

63

Personal Journal

All Scripture is God-breathed and is useful for teaching, rebuking, correcting and training in righteousness, so that the servant of God may be thoroughly equipped for every good work. **(2 Timothy 3:16-17)**

Take time to reflect and write about what you learned in this lesson as it relates to the Bible, What I Believe, and What is a Confession.

Below are a few reminders from lesson 7 to assist with your personal journal writing.

* The bible is a spiritual book consisting of God's laws for His people.
* The bible foretells the coming of the Messiah, Christ Jesus our Lord, His life, birth, death, resurrection and God's plan of salvation for my life.
* Some of the principle components of what I Believe

Prayer:

I open my heart to you dear God. I ask for wisdom and understanding. Please guide and teach me in knowledge and truth so I may live and grow stronger in my faith.

"...You are a part of the body of Christ.
God has chosen different ones in the church to do his work."
1 Corinthians 12:27-28

Personal Journal:

Summarize what you have learned in this lesson.

_____

_____

_____

_____

_____

_____

_____

_____

_____

How will this lesson impact your life?

_____

_____

_____

_____

_____

_____

_____

_____

_____

_____

"…You are a part of the body of Christ.
God has chosen different ones in the church to do his work."
1 Corinthians 12:27-28

65

LESSON VIII

THE MISSION-STATEMENTS OF FAITH MY-RESPONSIBILITY

The Mission, Statement of Faith, My Responsibility

Opening Song: I am not forgotten

Prayer: We thank You Father for giving us a church where we can gather together in love and fellowship. May we continue to live up to Your expectations and fulfill Your mission of meeting the needs of every human being. May our doors always be open to the young, the old, the rich and the poor, in every city, nation, and country around the world. Amen.

Scripture: *Jesus went through all the towns and villages, teaching in their synagogues, preaching the good news of the kingdom and healing, every disease and sickness. When he saw the crowds, he had compassion on them, because they were harassed and helpless, like sheep without a shepherd. Then he said to his disciples. The harvest is plentiful but the workers are few. Ask the Lord of the harvest, therefore, to send out workers into his harvest field.* **(Matthew 9:35-38)**

Purpose

The purpose of this lesson is to teach you about:

- The Mission
- Statements of Faith
- My Responsibility

Principle teaching: The principle teaching is to encourage youth to be responsible Christians and how they can give back to others.

Material Needed:

- PowerPoint screen
- Projector
- Paper
- Pens
- Magic markers
- Easel paper
- Prizes

Special Instructions: Students are encouraged to highlight scripture references in their Bibles and keep a personal journal. For each group exercise, divide students into small groups of 5-7.

My Confirmation Goal

My Christian journey thus far has been one that was decided for me when I was a child. I am no longer a child. I am now at the age where I must decide if I want to accept God's free gift of salvation and make it my own.

My parents, guardians and my church are here to help and guide me along this journey. However, the decision is now my responsibility. The instructions I receive during my confirmation classes will help me learn more about my faith.

While I am in the process of learning about my faith and how to be a Christian, I will not pretend to know all the answers. I am willing to learn all I can and to be all I can. I will give back to my church. I will live out my faith in my school, community and the world.

As a responsible youth my confirmation will give me the opportunity to become an active member of the church body.

My profession of faith will allow the Holy Spirit to begin a new work in me and confirm me into the church.

I affirm that my confirmation goal is to live out what my parents, guardians and church have accepted for me as an infant when I was baptized.

"…You are a part of the body of Christ.
God has chosen different ones in the church to do his work."
1 Corinthians 12:27-28

69

Exercise I

After reviewing the six (6) principles and nine (9) ways we fulfill the mission, divide students into their small groups. Assign each group one or more of the nine ways listed below to develop their own mission project.

(30 minutes)

The Nine Ways:

1. Preaching the gospel
2. Feeding the hungry
3. Clothing the naked
4. Providing housing to the homeless
5. Encouraging the fallen
6. Providing jobs to the jobless.
7. Administering to those in need
8. Caring for the sick
9. Encouraging economic advancement

Special Instructions

At the completion of their assignment, each group is to present their project to the class. The presentation can be written, a skit or a combination of both. In either case, each group must define the need for a mission project and the reason why they chose their method to respond to that particular need.

Journal

Have the students reflect and write in their journal:

1. Summarize what you have learned in this lesson.
2. How has this lesson impacted your life? **(5 minutes)**

Closing Prayer: Lord I thank You for giving me a greater appreciation for ministry. May my work represent Your love and compassion and be a blessing to others. Amen.

*"...You are a part of the body of Christ.
God has chosen different ones in the church to do his work."*
1 Corinthians 12:27-28

REW
MINISTRIES

TABLE OF CONTENTS

THE MISSION

- The mission is to minister to the spiritual, intellectual, physical and emotional needs of all people by spreading Christ's liberating gospel through word and deed.[8] **(See Matthew 28:16-20; Mark 6:7-13; Mark 1615)**

- Mission Statements are important. They help define and capture in simplicity the essence of a church mission and purpose.

"...You are a part of the body of Christ.
God has chosen different ones in the church to do his work."
1 Corinthians 12:27-28

71

THE SIX (6) PRINCIPLES OF A MISSION

The Mission is to minister to the:
1. Spiritual needs of all people
2. Intellectual needs of all people
3. Physical needs of all people
4. Emotional needs of all people
5. Environmental needs of all people
6. By spreading Christ's liberating gospel through word and deed.[9]

NINE (9) WAYS WE FULFILL A MISSION

1. By preaching the gospel
2. By feeding the hungry
3. By clothing the naked
4. By providing housing to the homeless
5. By encouraging the fallen, (being a voice to the voiceless)
6. By providing jobs for the jobless.
7. By administering to the needs of those in prisons, hospitals, nursing homes, senior citizens homes, asylums and mental institutions
8. By caring for the sick, the shut-in, the mentally and socially disturbed
9. By encouraging thrift and economic advancement.[10]
   (See Matthew 25:31-46)

*"...You are a part of the body of Christ.
God has chosen different ones in the church to do his work."*
1 Corinthians 12:27-28

STATEMENTS OF FAITH

THE TRINITY

For there are three that testify: the Spirit, the water and the blood; and the three are in agreement. **(1 John 5:7-8)**

- The three personas of the One and Only God: The Father, Son and Holy Spirit is called the Trinity

STATEMENTS OF FAITH

JESUS IS THE INCARNATED WORD OF GOD

The Word became flesh and made his dwelling among us. We have seen his glory, the glory of the One and Only, who came from the Father, full of grace and truth. **(John 1:14)**

"…You are a part of the body of Christ.
God has chosen different ones in the church to do his work."
1 Corinthians 12:27-28

73

STATEMENTS OF FAITH

THE RESURRECTION OF CHRIST

- *Christ truly rose from the dead and ascended into heaven.* **(Matthew 28:1-7; Mark 16:1-6; Luke 24:1-6; John 20:1-13; 1 Corinthians 15:3-4)**
  - *After the Lord Jesus had spoken to them, he was taken up into heaven and he sat at the right hand of God.* **(Mark 15:19)**
  - *When he had led them out to the vicinity of Bethany he lifted up his hands and blessed them. While he was blessing them, he left them and was taken up to heaven.* **(Luke 24:50)**

STATEMENTS OF FAITH

THE HOLY SPIRIT

- The Holy Spirit is one substance with the Father and the Son, the third part of the Trinity.
  - *When the Counselor comes, whom I will send to you from the Father, the Spirit of truth who goes out from the Father, he will testify about me.* **(John 15:26)**

"…You are a part of the body of Christ.
God has chosen different ones in the church to do his work."
1 Corinthians 12:27-28

STATEMENTS OF FAITH

THE HOLY SCRIPTURES

- The Holy Scriptures is the inspired word of God.
  - *All Scripture is God-breathed and is useful for teaching, rebuking, correcting, and Training in righteousness, so that the servant of God may be thoroughly equipped for every good work.* **(2 Timothy 3:16:17)**

STATEMENTS OF FAITH

THE OLD TESTAMENT AND NEW TESTAMENT

- In both the Old and New Testaments, eternal life is offered to humankind by Christ, who is the only mediator between God and man.

"...You are a part of the body of Christ.
God has chosen different ones in the church to do his work."
1 Corinthians 12:27-28

75

STATEMENTS OF FAITH

OUR SINFUL NATURE

- This corruption of the nature of every human being is called "original or birth sin". **(Genesis 3:1-24)**

STATEMENTS OF FAITH

FREE WILL

- While we have the liberty to act at our own discretion,
  We have no power to do good works, pleasant and acceptable to God, without the grace of God and the good will of Christ working within us. **(Ephesians 2:8-9)**

"...You are a part of the body of Christ.
God has chosen different ones in the church to do his work."
1 Corinthians 12:27-28

STATEMENTS OF FAITH

Know that a man is not justified by observing the law, but by faith in Jesus Christ, so we too have put our faith in Christ Jesus that we may be justified by faith in Christ and not by observing the law, because by observing the law no one will be justified. **(Galatians 2:16)**

THE JUSTIFICATION OF MAN

- We are accounted righteous before God only through our Lord and Savior Jesus Christ. It is by faith, and not by our own works. We are justified only by faith.[11]
  - *For it is by grace you have been saved, through faith—and this is not from yourselves, it is a gift of God.* **(Ephesians 2:8)**
  - *For all have sinned and fall short of the glory of God, and are justified freely by his grace through the redemption that came by Christ Jesus.* **(Roman 3:23-24)**

STATEMENTS OF FAITH

Let your light so shine before men, that they may see your good works, and glorify your Father which is in heaven. **(Matthew 5:16)**

GOOD WORKS

- Good works are the fruits of our faith; they cannot put away our sins and endure the severity of God's judgments. Yet, they are pleasing and acceptable to God in Christ.[12]

REW
MINISTRIES

"…You are a part of the body of Christ.
God has chosen different ones in the church to do his work."
1 Corinthians 12:27-28

77

STATEMENTS OF FAITH

*If we confess our sins, he is faithful and just and will forgive us our
sins and purify us from all unrighteousness.* **(1 John 1:9)**

SIN AFTER JUSTIFICATION

- After we have received the Holy Ghost, we may depart from grace given, and fall
  into sin, and by the grace of God, rise again, and amend our lives.[13]

STATEMENTS OF FAITH

THE CHURCH

- The visible Church of Christ is a congregation of faithful men and women in which
  the pure Word of God is preached, and the Sacraments duly administered according
  to Christ's ordinance.[14]

*"...You are a part of the body of Christ.
God has chosen different ones in the church to do his work."*
1 Corinthians 12:27-28

STATEMENTS OF FAITH

SPEAKING IN TONGUES

- Public worship and the sacraments should be conducted in a language the people can understand. **(see 1 Corinthians 14:2-28)**

STATEMENTS OF FAITH

THE SACRAMENTS

- There are two sacraments in the Gospels (Matthew, Mark, Luke and John) ordained of Christ: Baptism and the Lord's Supper or Holy Communion.

"...You are a part of the body of Christ.
God has chosen different ones in the church to do his work."
1 Corinthians 12:27-28

79

STATEMENTS OF FAITH

Jesus answered, "I tell you the truth, no one can enter the kingdom of God unless he is born of water and the Spirit. **(John 3:5)**

BAPTISM

- Baptism is not only a sign of our profession, and mark of our difference; but it is also a sign of regeneration or the new birth.[15]
- **(John 3:3-5; Romans 6:3-4)**
- Baptism marks the beginning of the Christian life.

STATEMENTS OF FAITH

THE LORD'S SUPPER/HOLY COMMUNION

- The Lord's Supper is a symbol of Christ's suffering and death.
  The bread and wine represent his broken body and shed blood. **(Matthew 26:17-30; Mark 14:12-26; Luke 22:7-20; 1 Corinthians 11:17-26)**

"...You are a part of the body of Christ.
God has chosen different ones in the church to do his work."
1 Corinthians 12:27-28

STATEMENTS OF FAITH

BOTH THE BREAD AND THE WINE ARE SACRAMENTS OF ONE FAITH

- *While they were eating, Jesus took bread, and when he had given thanks, he broke it and gave it to his disciples, saying, "Take and eat; this is my body." Then he took a cup, and when he had given thanks, he gave it to them, saying, "Drink from it, all of you. This is my blood of the covenant, which is poured out for many for the forgiveness of sins.* **(Matthew 26:26-28)**

STATEMENTS OF FAITH

God made him who had no sin to be sin for us, so that in him we might become the righteousness of God. **(2 Corinthians 5:21)**

THE SACRIFICE OF CHRIST

- The sacrifice of Christ is for the sins of the whole world, both original and actual. There is no other satisfaction for sin but that alone.[16]
  - *But God demonstrates his own love for us in this; While we were still sinners, Christ died for us.* **(Romans 5:8)**

*"...You are a part of the body of Christ.
God has chosen different ones in the church to do his work."*
1 Corinthians 12:27-28

81

MY RESPONSIBILITY

GOOD STEWARD

He save us, not because of righteous things we have done, but because of his mercy. He saved us through the washing of rebirth and renewal by the Holy Spirit, whom he poured out on us generously through Jesus Christ our Savior, so that, having been justified by his grace, we might become heirs having the hope of eternal life. **(Titus 3:5-7)**

- My "confirmation" can be seen literally as a turning point in my life. In the process of my spiritual transformation, I can experience God's grace and mercy over my life through justification, regeneration and adoption.

MY RESPONSIBILITY

GOOD STEWARD

Salvation requires that I take personal responsibility over my life. When I accept God's free gift of salvation, it is now my responsibility as a good steward to witness and encourage others to do the same. **(See Matthew 28:18-19)**

If you confess with your mouth Jesus as Lord, and believe in your heart that God raised Him from the dead, you shall be saved. **(Romans 10:9)**

- When I take responsibility, I can be rescued by God and enter into a union with other believers.

"...You are a part of the body of Christ.
God has chosen different ones in the church to do his work."
1 Corinthians 12:27-28

MY RESPONSIBILITY

GOOD STEWARD

Again, it will be like a man going on a journey, who called his servants and entrusted his property to them. To one he gave five talents of money, to another two talents, and to another one talent, each according to his ability. Then he went on his journey. **(Matthew 25:14-15)**

- A **steward** is a manager over all that belongs to God.
- As a **steward,** God has entrusted me with special gifts, talents and abilities to be used for His glory.
- A **steward** serves God out of love and gratitude for these gifts, talents and abilities. It is not how much we have, but what we do with what we have.

MY RESPONSIBILITY

STEWARDSHIP

God blessed them and said to them, "Be fruitful and increase in number; fill the earth and subdue it. Rule over the fish of the sea and the birds of the air and over every living creature that moves on the ground. **(Genesis 1:28)**

- No book of the bible is more important to our understanding of stewardship than the book of Genesis. It is in Genesis that God outlines our roles and responsibilities for Stewardship. God's ultimate desire is that we be responsible stewards over the land, sea, air and everything create in the beginning of time.
- Stewardship requires management responsibility, dependability and accountability to God of our time, talent and the treasures of life entrusted in our care.

"...You are a part of the body of Christ.
God has chosen different ones in the church to do his work."
1 Corinthians 12:27-28

83

MY RESPONSIBILITY

TIME

Teach us to number our days aright, that we may gain a heart of wisdom **(Psalm 90:12)**

- When God gives us life, we do not know how much time we have here on earth.
- Whatever time we have, we must mange it wisely.
- We must budget our time to fulfill God's will for our lives and too accomplish our goals and objectives.

MY RESPONSIBILITY

TALENTS

Well done good and faithful servant. You have been faithful with a few things; I will put you in charge of many things . . . **(Matthew 25:21)**

- **Talents are distributed according to our ability through the providential will of God.**
    - *Let us not become weary in doing good, for at the proper time we will reap a harvest if we do not give up. Therefore, as we have opportunity let us do good to all people, especially to those who belong to the family of believers.* **(Galatians 6:9-10)**

"...You are a part of the body of Christ.
God has chosen different ones in the church to do his work."
1 Corinthians 12:27-28

MY RESPONSIBILITY

TREASURES

When they arrived at the house of the Lord in Jerusalem, some of the heads of the families gave freewill offerings towards the rebuilding of the house of God on its site. According to their ability they gave to the treasury for this work . . . **(Ezra 2:68-69)**

- Offerings are another form of giving.
- Offerings are free-will gifts.
- No one can tell you what to give, however, giving back to God in tithes and offerings is an expression of your love and commitment.

MY RESPONSIBILITY

TREASURES

Then they faithfully brought in the contributions, tithes and dedicated gifts . . . **(2 Chronicles 31:12)**

- A tithe or tithing is the act of giving one-tenth of a person's treasure. It is our response to give back to God what we have been blessed to have received from God. *Then Abram gave him a tenth of everything.* **(Genesis 14:20)**

Offerings are also a response to God's blessings. Offerings are not meant to replace a tithe, but to give in addition to a tithe.

*"...You are a part of the body of Christ.
God has chosen different ones in the church to do his work."*
1 Corinthians 12:27-28

85

MY RESPONSIBILITY

TREASURES

"God is rich in money and love and has showered his riches on us"
He has given us the incomparable riches of His grace, expressed in His kindness to us in Christ Jesus. **(Ephesians 2:7)**

- As a responsible Christian, I understand that giving of my tithes and offerings is required of me to support the ongoing ministries of my local church in sharing the Gospel of Jesus Christ. **(Deuteronomy 26:1-4; Malachi 3:10; Acts 4:32-35)**
- On the first day of the week let each of you lay something aside, storing up as he may prosper. **(1 Corinthians 16:2)**

MY RESPONSIBILITY

TREASURES

Honor the Lord with your possessions and with the first fruits of all your increase; so your barns will be filled with plenty, and your vats will overflow with new wine. **(Proverbs 3:9-10)**

- I understand as a responsible member, when I make every effort to be faithful to God and to my church through the giving of my tithes and offerings, I too will be blessed.
- *Bring all the tithes into the storehouse, that there may be food in My house, and try Me now in this, says the Lord of hosts, "If I will not open for you the windows of heaven and pour out for you such a blessing that there will not be room enough to receive it.* **(Malachi 3:10)**

*"...You are a part of the body of Christ.
God has chosen different ones in the church to do his work."*
1 Corinthians 12:27-28

MY RESPONSIBILITY

TREASURES

- Giving is an honor and a privilege.
  - *In the midst of a very severe trial, their overflowing joy, and their extreme poverty welled up in rich generosity. For I testify that they gave as much as they were able, and even beyond their ability. Entirely on their own, they urgently pleaded with us for the privilege of sharing in this service to the Lord's people.* **(2 Corinthians 8:2-4)**

*"…You are a part of the body of Christ.
God has chosen different ones in the church to do his work."*
1 Corinthians 12:27-28

87

Personal Journal

Then he said to his disciples. The harvest is plentiful but the workers are few.
(Matthew 9:38)

**Take time to reflect and write about what you learned in
this lesson as it relates to My Responsibility.**

Below are a few reminders from lesson 8 to assist with your personal journal writing:

* My responsibility is to share the good news and to bring God's message to a dying world.
* I will take my responsibility seriously and help others to believe in the Name of Jesus
* I will be a responsible Christians through my words, deeds and acts.

Prayer:
Dear God, I will never forget the precious gift of Jesus Christ. I promise to be a
responsible Christian. May all my work bring glory and honor to your name. Amen.

*"…You are a part of the body of Christ.
God has chosen different ones in the church to do his work."*
1 Corinthians 12:27-28

Personal Journal:

Summarize what you have learned in this lesson.

_____

_____

_____

_____

_____

_____

_____

_____

_____

_____

How will this lesson impact your life?

_____

_____

_____

_____

_____

_____

_____

_____

_____

_____

_____

"…You are a part of the body of Christ.
God has chosen different ones in the church to do his work."
1 Corinthians 12:27-28

89

HANDOUT 1

Date:

To: The Parents/Guardians of _____

From:

Subject: Youth Confirmation Classes

During the next several weeks beginning on _____, through _____, I am encouraging you to enroll your youth ages 13-18 in a eight week two-hour confirmation lesson series.

During these weeks the focus is to help youth:

- discover new insights about Christian beliefs
- the Church doctrine and traditions
- role and responsibility as Christians

This is a great opportunity to share what we believe and to help youth find meaning and purpose in their faith. It is also my prayer that you as parents/guardians will support your youth throughout this spiritual journey.

In Christ's Service,

Pastor

"...You are a part of the body of Christ.
God has chosen different ones in the church to do his work."
1 Corinthians 12:27-28

HANDOUT 2—Confirmation Schedule

Date	1. **Lesson I** • Defining Confirmation • Confirmation Goal • Building Community • Your Decision on Becoming a Disciple of Christ • Questionnaire I
Date	2. **Lesson II** • The Trinity • God the Son • God the Father • God the Holy Spirit
Date	3. **Lesson III** • Jesus is the Son of God • Jesus is the Christ • Jesus is the Savior of the World
Date	4. **Lesson IV** • The Holy Spirit • Life in the Spirit • Fruit of the Spirit
Date	5. **Lesson V** • Defining Salvation • Act of Confession • Personal Salvation
Date	6. **Lesson VI** • Defining Worship • The Way We Worship • How We Worship • Worship Terms and Definitions • Where We Worship
Date	7. **Session VII** • The Bible • What I Believe • The General Confession
Date	8. **Session VIII** • The Mission • Statements of Faith • My Responsibility • Final Questionnaire • Final Preparation for Confirmation

"...You are a part of the body of Christ.
God has chosen different ones in the church to do his work."
1 Corinthians 12:27-28

91

HANDOUT 3

Questionnaire I (circle one answer for each question)

Gender_____ Student#_____ Age_____

1. How would you use your knowledge to explain to a non-believer the Bible is the true and inspired Word of God?
   a. God chose angels to translate in every language what He wanted us to know and learn.
   b. All Scripture is God-breathed and is useful for teaching, rebuking, connecting and training in righteousness.
   c. In the beginning of time God sat down and wrote every word and gave them to us to read.

2. If you knew your best friend was about to make a wrong decision, how would you use your Christian beliefs, knowledge and values to help your friend?
   a. Ask your pastor to pray for them.
   b. Invite them to a Christian movie.
   c. By demonstrating the fruit of the Spirit.

3. Explain how having knowledge about the Bible would be helpful in your own spiritual development.
   a. Reading my Bible every day, especially on Sundays before I go to church.
   b. It helps me to understand Christ Jesus our Lord, His life, birth, death, resurrection and God's plan of salvation.
   c. It has great stories of people who lived in the past.

4. Tim is into drugs and gangs. Explain how you would lead Tim to Christ Jesus.
   a. Show Tim why we need Jesus in our lives and in the world.
   b. Tell Tim if he continues doing wrong, he will most likely get in trouble and go to jail.
   c. Convince Tim that if he does not stop, you will have to report him to his parents.

5. Explain how your knowledge about salvation, faith and baptism would help someone struggling with depression and poor self esteem.
   a. Tell them about the power of positive thinking.
   b. Give advice on how to dress and act so people will like them.
   c. Explain how confirmation works.

6. Explain how different styles of music enhances the church service and church growth.
   a. It encourages others to praise God and allows people to sing, dance and pray in various ways.
   b. Worship should not have to change to make the church grow.
   c. The pastor in charge, not the music, determines the need for church growth.

7. Explain why your involvement in a ministry that helps the poor and the homeless would be important for your spiritual growth.
   a. Individual involvement in a ministry does not impact spiritual growth.
   b. Involvement in a ministry helps to serve God out of love and gratitude for what God has done for each of us.
   c. Personal growth is only measured by how much you know about the Bible.

8. Explain the Trinity
   a. The Trinity is when you have three of the same things.
   b. The Trinity is God in three different persons.
   c. The Trinity is the three aspects or personas of God.

"...You are a part of the body of Christ.
God has chosen different ones in the church to do his work."
1 Corinthians 12:27-28

HANDOUT 4

Final Questionnaire (circle one answer for each question)

Gender_____ Student#_____ Age_____

1. How would you use your knowledge to explain to a non-believer that the Bible is the true and inspired Word of God?
   a. God chose angels to translate in every language what He wanted us to know and learn.
   b. All Scripture is God-breathed and is useful for teaching, rebuking, connecting and training in righteousness.
   c. In the beginning of time God sat down and wrote every word and gave them to us to read.

2. If you knew your best friend was about to make a wrong decision, how would you use your Christian beliefs, knowledge, and values to help your friend?
   a. Ask your pastor to pray for them.
   b. Invite them to a Christian movie.
   c. By demonstrating the fruit of the Spirit.

3. Explain how having knowledge about the Bible would be helpful in your own spiritual development.
   a. Reading my Bible every day, especially on Sundays before I go to church.
   b. It helps me to understand Christ Jesus our Lord, His life, birth, death, resurrection and God's plan of salvation.
   c. It has great stories of people who lived in the past.

4. Tim is into drugs and gang activity. Explain how you would lead Tim to Christ.
   a. Show Tim why we need Jesus in our lives and in the world.
   b. Tell Tim if he continues doing wrong, he will most likely get in trouble and go to jail.
   c. Tell Tim that if he does not stop, you will have to report him to his parents.

5. Explain how your knowledge about salvation, faith, and baptism would help someone struggling with depression and poor self esteem.
   a. Tell them about the power of positive thinking.
   b. Give advice on how to dress and act so people will like them.
   c. Explain how confirmation works.

6. Explain how different styles of music enhances the church service and church growth.
   a. It encourages others to praise God and allows people to sing, dance and pray in various ways.
   b. Worship should not have to change to make the church grow.
   c. The pastor in charge, not the music, determines the need for church growth.

7. Explain why your involvement in a ministry that helps the poor and the homeless would be important for your spiritual growth.
   a. Individual involvement in a ministry does not impact spiritual growth.
   b. Involvement in a ministry helps to serve God out of love and gratitude for what God has done for each of us.
   c. Personal growth is only measured by how much you know about the Bible.

8. Explain the Trinity
   a. The Trinity is when you have three of the same things.
   b. The Trinity is God in three different persons.
   c. The Trinity is the three aspects or personas of God.

*"...You are a part of the body of Christ.
God has chosen different ones in the church to do his work."*
1 Corinthians 12:27-28

93

HANDOUT 5

What is Confirmation?

1. Confirmation is another way of saying we confirm our faith belief. It is the act of verifying or confirming what we have been taught by our parents and our church as it relates to God and our relationship with Christ Jesus.

2. In our faith tradition, many of us were baptized long before we had the opportunity to understand the meaning of our baptism.

   When we were baptized, our parents or guardians took a vow and agreed to accept the responsibility to see that we were taught the nature and the meaning of our baptism.

   The church also stood in agreement to help teach us such things as the Lord's Prayer, the Ten Commandments, the meaning of our Christian faith and all the things a Christian should know.

3. We believe that baptism is a sacrament ordained of Christ. Our baptism is not only a profession of our faith, it is also a sign of God's grace and good will towards us.

4. Confirmation is about a personal acceptance and acknowledgment of God's grace and love for us through the free gift of salvation through Jesus Christ.

   The Bible tells us, "God so loved the world that he gave his One and Only Son." (John 3:16 NIV) As a result of God's gift to the world, our parents or guardians accepted the gift of Christ for us on the day we were baptized.

Although the gift is free, we have the right to accept it or to reject it. Confirmation gives us that opportunity to make the decision and decide for ourselves if we want this gift from God and to "confirm" what was accepted for us by our parents, guardians and the church.

5. As youth, we are now at the age where we can decide for ourselves about our salvation.

6. While our parents and the church will be there to help and guide us along this journey, it is now our own responsibility and God requires each of us to make our own decision.

7. We are more mentally prepared to comprehend and learn about what it means to be a Christian and active member of the body of Christ. We are also old enough to learn what we believe: our doctrine, discipline, history, heritage and how we are to live as Christians.

8. While we may not have the answers to all the questions, with God on our side and the Spirit of the Lord to guide us, we can learn along the way.

9. We are old enough where others will know we made a decision for ourselves and confirmed before God and the church what we believe. Our confirmation gives us an active voice where we can now live out our faith in our church, school, community and in the world.

"...You are a part of the body of Christ.
God has chosen different ones in the church to do his work."
1 Corinthians 12:27-28

HANDOUT 6

Your Decision on Becoming a Disciple of Christ

1.	During this confirmation process, you will have a unique opportunity to make a decision to become a disciple of Christ. When the invitation is given, It is our hope that you will respond and be confirmed on Confirmation Sunday.
2.	You do not have to be confirmed. The decision will be entirely yours. You may decide now or at a later time. However, it is our hope that you will accept the invitation to Christian discipleship at the time of confirmation. Choosing not to be confirmed does not affect your ability to participate in the church or in any activities at your church.
3.	If you have been baptized, we affirm your baptism and there is no need to be re-baptized.
4.	If you have not been baptized, you will be given an opportunity to be baptized following your response to accept Jesus Christ as your Lord and Savior. Baptism is the gateway into the body of Christ, a particular denomination and local church.
5.	Confirmation is done with your confession and a prayer that the Holy Spirit will continue to work in your life. If you choose to be confirmed, you will become an active member of the body of Christ with all rights and privileges to the kingdom of God.
6.	While you may complete these classes, confirmation is not the end. It is the beginning of a lifelong journey together with the Lord. Confirmation will build on the values your parents have taught you, what you have learned in the church and your personal experiences with God.
7.	Our prayer is that you will take this confirmation process seriously. Everything in these classes is important. "No part is optional, your attendance is vital." You must make a decision to be regular in attendance. When you make this decision, you will experience the power of the Holy Spirit working in your life like never before.
8.	When you are confirmed, you are making a public profession before your family, church and friends that you are now a part of the body of Christ!

"...You are a part of the body of Christ.
God has chosen different ones in the church to do his work."
1 Corinthians 12:27-28

95

HANDOUT 7

The Trinity Handout

The word "Trinity" does not appear in the Bible; it is a theological term used to describe the three members of the Godhead.

1. The Trinity is defined as the three personas of God: • God the Father • God the Son • God the Holy Spirit	2. "Tri" meaning three, and "Unity" meaning one, Tri + Unity = Trinity. It is a way of acknowledging what the Bible reveals to us about God, that God is yet three "Persons" who have the same essence of deity.
3. Three personas of the One and Only God can be found in the following scripture. (Matthew 28:19)	4. There is but one living and true God. He is the maker and preserver of all things. We experience the one God through three aspects of His personality: the Father, Son and Holy Spirit.
5. The Father as the source of creation, the giver of life, and God of all the universe. (Genesis 1:1-31; 2:1 and John 1:1-3; 1 Corinthians. 8:6; Ephesians 3:14-15; Hebrews 1:1-2)	6. In Christ there are two natures: one is divine and the other is human. They are joined together in one person. This is what is meant by God incarnated. (John 1:14; 1 Timothy 3:16)
7. The Son is depicted as the image of the invisible God, the exact representation of his being and nature, the Messiah—Redeemer. (John 1:14; Philippians 2:5-6; Colossians 1:14-16; Hebrews 1: 3)	8. The life giving Spirit is the Holy Spirit. When Jesus ascended into heaven, (Luke 24:29) his physical presence left the earth. He promised to send the Holy Spirit so that his spiritual presence would always be with us. (John 14:15; John 14:26).
9. The Spirit is God in action, God reaching people-influencing them, regenerating them, infilling them and guiding them. (John 14:26; John 16:13-15; Acts 2:2-4)	10. The symbol that best describes the Trinity is a triangle.
11. All three are a tri-unity, inhabiting one another and working together to accomplish the divine design in the universe. (John 16:13-15)[17]	12. God the Father ⟋⟍ God the Son God the Holy Spirit **All three in One**

"...You are a part of the body of Christ.
God has chosen different ones in the church to do his work."
1 Corinthians 12:27-28

HANDOUT 8

God Is
Exercise III—Handout

Instructions:

Using your NIV Bibles find the following ten scriptures:

(Psalm 7:11; 1 Corinthians 10:13; Hebrew 3:4; 2 Chronicles 30:9; Psalm 54:4; Daniel 9:9; 2 Samuel 22:3; Job 36:5; Deuteronomy 4:24; Psalm 84:11)

You are to identify and write out the scripture with the entire verse that best describes the characteristics of God listed below:

1. consuming fire; jealous God
    * _____

2. rock, salvation, stronghold, refuge, savior
    * _____

3. gracious and compassionate
    * _____

4. mighty
    * _____

5. judge
    * _____

6. help
    * _____

7. sun and shield
    * _____

8. merciful and forgiving
    * _____

9. faithful
    * _____

10. builder
    * _____

"...You are a part of the body of Christ.
God has chosen different ones in the church to do his work."
1 Corinthians 12:27-28

97

HANDOUT 9

Jesus Is
Exercise III—Handout

Using your NIV Bibles:

- Find the scriptures listed below.
- List the one word that best describes the characteristics of Jesus.
- Complete the sentence.
- The scripture reference should be placed at the end of the sentence.
  (John 15:1; John 11:25; John 10:9; John 14:6; John 6:35; John 8:12; John 10:11)

1. _____
   "I am the _____ of life; Whoever comes to me will never _____, and whoever believes in me will never be_____ _____".

2. _____
   "I am the _____ of the world: Whoever follows me will never walk in darkness, but will have _____ of life". _____

3. _____
   "I am the _____; whoever enters through me will be saved. They will come in and go _____ _____

   and find _____" _____

4. _____
   "I am the good _____; the good _____ lays down His life for His _____". _____

5. _____
   "I am the _____ and the _____; he who believes in Me will _____ even if they die". _____

6. _____
   "I am the _____, and the _____, and the _____ No one comes to the Father, except through Me". _____

7. _____
   "I am the _____, and My Father is the gardener". _____

"...You are a part of the body of Christ.
God has chosen different ones in the church to do his work."
1 Corinthians 12:27-28

HANDOUT 9A

Jesus Is
Exercise I—Answer Sheet

Using your NIV Bibles:

- Find the scriptures listed below.
- List the one word that best describes the characteristic of Jesus.
- Complete the sentence.
  (John 15:1; John 11:25; John 10:9; John 14:6; John 6:35; John 8:12; John 10:11)

1. **Bread**
   "Then Jesus declared, "I am the bread of life. Whoever comes to me will never go hungry, and whoever believes in me will never be thirsty". **(John 6:35)**

2. **Light**
   "When Jesus spoke again to the people, he said, "I am the light of the world. Whoever follows me will never walk in darkness, but will have the light of life". **(John 8:12)**

3. **Gate**
   "I am the gate; whoever enters through me will be saved. They will come in and go out, and find pasture". **(John 10:9)**

4. **Good Shepherd**
   "I am the good shepherd: the good shepherd lays down His life for His sheep". **(John 10:11)**

5. **Resurrection and Life**
   "Jesus said to her, "I am the resurrection and the life. The one who believes in me will live, even though they die". **(John 11:25)**

6. **Way, Truth, Life**
   "Jesus answered, "I am the way and the truth and the life. No one comes to the Father except through me". **(John 14:6)**

7. **True vine**
   "I am the true vine, and my Father is the gardener". **(John 15:1)**

"...You are a part of the body of Christ.
God has chosen different ones in the church to do his work."
1 Corinthians 12:27-28

99

HANDOUT 10

The Holy Spirit
Exercise I—Handout

Using your NIV Bibles:

- Find the scriptures listed below.
- Then finish completing the sentence.
  (1 Corinthians 12:13; Ephesians 4:30; Romans 8:16; Titus 3:5; John 16:13; Romans 8:14; Ephesians 5:18; Romans 8:26)

1. Scripture _____
   - For we were all _____ Spirit so as to form one body whether Jews or Gentiles, slave or free and we were all given the _____ Spirit to drink.

2. Scripture _____
   - And do not grieve the _____ of God, with whom you were sealed for the day of redemption.

3. Scripture _____
   - The Spirit himself testifies with _____ spirit that we are _____
     .

4. Scripture _____
   - He saved us, not because of righteous things we had done, but because of his mercy. He saved us through the washing of _____ by the Holy Spirit.

5. Scripture _____
   - In the same way, the Spirit _____ us in _____. We do not know what we ought to pray for, but _____ himself _____ for _____ us through wordless groans.

6. Scripture _____
   - But when he, _____, comes, he will guide you into all the truth. He will not speak on his own; he will speak only what he hears, and he will tell you what is yet to come.

7. Scripture _____
   - For those who are _____ the Spirit of God are the _____.

8. Scripture _____
   Do not get drunk on wine, which leads to debauchery. Instead, _____ with the Spirit . . .

"...You are a part of the body of Christ.
God has chosen different ones in the church to do his work."
1 Corinthians 12:27-28

HANDOUT 10A

The Holy Spirit
Exercise I—Answer Sheet

Using your NIV Bibles:

- Find the scriptures listed below.
- Then finish completing the sentence.
  (Romans 8:16; Titus 3:5; Ephesians 5:18; Romans 8:14; 1 Corinthians 12:13; John 16:13; Ephesians 4:30; Romans 8:26).

1. **Corinthians 12:13**
   - For we were all **baptized by one** Spirit so as to form one body whether Jews or Gentiles, slave or free and we were all given the **one** Spirit to drink.

2. **Ephesians 4:30**
   - And do not grieve the **Holy Spirit** of God, with whom you were sealed for the day of redemption.

3. **Romans 8:16**
   - The Spirit himself testifies with **our** spirit that we are **God's children.**

4. **Titus 3:5**
   - He saved us, not because of righteous things we had done, but because of his mercy. He saved us through the washing of **rebirth and renewal** by the Holy Spirit,

5. **Romans 8:26**
   - In the same way, the Spirit **helps** us in **our weakness.** We do not know what we ought to pray for, but **the Spirit** himself **intercedes** for us through wordless groans.

6. **John 16:13**
   - But when he, the **Spirit of truth,** comes, he will guide you into all the truth. He will not speak on his own; he will speak only what he hears, and he will tell you what is yet to come.

7. **Romans 8:14**
   - For those who are **led by** the Spirit of God are the **children of God.**

8. **Ephesians 5:18**
   - Do not get drunk on wine, which leads to debauchery. Instead, **be filled** with the Spirit . . .

"...You are a part of the body of Christ.
God has chosen different ones in the church to do his work."
1 Corinthians 12:27-28

101

HANDOUT 11

Fruit of the Spirit—Handout

The fruit of the Spirit are nine biblical characteristics produced within us by the Holy Spirit that defines a believer's life in Jesus Christ. These characteristics are "love, joy, peace, patience, kindness, goodness, faithfulness, gentleness and self-control". (Galatians 5:22-23). These characteristics are not individual fruit working independently of one another, but collectively working together in us signifying that we are representing the body of Christ.

1. **Love**—"The greatest of these is love, **(1 Corinthians 13:12)** our goal as Christians is to do all things with the love of Christ. "As God has loved us we are to love one another." **(John 13:14)** "Love is patient, love is kind. It does not envy, it does not boast, it is not proud. It is not rude, it is not self-seeking, it is not easily angered, it keeps no record of wrongs. Love does not delight in evil but rejoices with the truth. It always protects, always trusts, always hopes, always perseveres. Love never fails." **(1 Corinthians 13:4-8)**

2. **Joy**—"The joy of the Lord is your strength." **(Nehemiah 8:10)** "Let us fix our eyes on Jesus, the author and perfecter of our faith, who for the joy set before him endured the cross, scorning its shame, and sat down at the right hand of the throne of God." **(Hebrews 12:2)**

3. **Peace**—"Therefore, since we have been justified through faith, we have peace with God through our Lord Jesus Christ." **(Romans 5:1)** "May the God of hope fill you with all joy and peace as you trust in him, so that you may overflow with hope by the power of the Holy Spirit." **(Romans 15:13)**

4. **Patience**—We are "strengthened with all might, according to his glorious power, unto all patience and long suffering with joyfulness." **(Colossians 1:11),** "With all lowliness and meekness, with long suffering, forbearing one another in love. **(Ephesians. 4:2)**

5. **Kindness**—We should live "in purity, understanding, patience and kindness; in the Holy Spirit and in sincere love; in truthful speech and in the power of God; with weapons of righteousness in the right hand and in the left." **(2 Corinthians 6:6-7)**

6. **Goodness**—"Wherefore also we pray always for you, that our God would count you worthy of this calling, and fulfill all the good pleasure of his goodness, and the work of faith with power." **(2 Thessalonians 1:11)** "For the fruit of the Spirit is in all goodness and righteousness and truth." **(Ephesians 5:9)**

7. **Faithfulness**—"O Lord, thou art my God; I will exalt thee, I will praise thy name; for thou hast done wonderful things; thy counsels of old are faithfulness and truth." **(Isaiah 25:1)** I pray that out of his glorious riches he may strengthen you with power through his Spirit in your inner being, so that Christ may dwell in your hearts through faith". **(Ephesians 3:16-17)**

8. **Gentleness**—"Therefore, as God's chosen people, holy and dearly loved, clothe yourselves with compassion, kindness, humility, gentleness and patience." **(Colossians 3:12)** "Be completely humble and gentle; be patient, bearing with one another in love." **(Ephesians 4:2)**

9. **Self-control**—"For this very reason, make every effort to add to your faith, goodness; and to goodness, knowledge; and to knowledge, self-control; and to self-control, perseverance; and to perseverance, godliness." **(2 Peter 1:5-7)**

"...You are a part of the body of Christ.
God has chosen different ones in the church to do his work."
1 Corinthians 12:27-28

HANDOUT 12

Salvation—Answer Sheet

Exercise I

- **John 6:37,** List the two promises given by Jesus:
  a. Whoever comes to me.
  b. I will never drive away.

- **John 10:28-29,** List the four promises of Jesus:
  a. I give them eternal life, and they shall never perish;
  b. No one will snatch them out of my hand.
  c. My Father, who has given them to me, is greater than all;
  d. No one can snatch them out of my Father's hand.

- **Ephesians 2:8,** name the two things that confirms our salvation:
  a. Grace
  b. Faith
- **Ephesians 2:9,** what are the two things that I can do to earn my salvation?
  a. Nothing
  b. It is a gift

Ten ways your salvation is secured. Romans 8:38-39.

1. **Death**
    - You cannot loose your salvation through death.
2. **Life**
    - You cannot loose your salvation while you are alive.
3. **Angels**
    - Angels have no power over your salvation.
4. **Demons**
    - Demons cannot take your salvation away.
5. **Present**
    - There is nothing in this present life that can take your salvation from you.
6. **Future**
    - No matter what happens in the future, your salvation will not change.
7. **Powers**
    - There are no powers strong enough to remove your salvation.
8. **Height**
    - There is nothing above you that can prevent your salvation.
9. **Depth**
    - There is nothing below you that can get beneath your salvation.
10. **Nor anything**
    - There is not anything in all creation that shall be able to separate us from the love of God, that is in Christ Jesus our Lord.

"…You are a part of the body of Christ.
God has chosen different ones in the church to do his work."
1 Corinthians 12:27-28

103

HANDOUT 13

Youth Confirmation Commitment

Pastor: I present to you this Bible which is the Word of God. Throughout the pages of your Bible you have underlined important scriptures from your course of study that will help you in many life situations. I pray that you use these scriptures and do your best to "present yourself to God as one approved, a workman who does not need to be ashamed and who correctly handles the word of truth." **(2 Timothy 2:15)**

Confirmands: This is my desire.

Pastor: I encourage you, "Do not let this Book of the Law depart from your mouth; meditate on it day and night, so that you may be careful to do everything written in it. Then you will be prosperous and successful." **(Joshua 1:8)**

Confirmands: This is my desire.

Pastor: As children of God, I understand that "the wages of sin is death and the gift of God is eternal life in Christ Jesus our Lord." (Romans 6:23). "Therefore, I urge you, brothers and sisters, in view of God's mercy, to offer your bodies as living sacrifices, holy and pleasing to God—this is your spiritual act of worship." **(Romans 12:1)**

Confirmands: This is my desire, God being my helper.

Pastor: Now that I know what is expected of me as a Christian, I will seek to live a life of "love, joy, peace, patience, kindness, goodness, faithfulness, gentleness and self-control." **(Galatians 5:22-23)**

Confirmands: This is my desire, God being my helper.

Pastor: I believe in God the Father Almighty, the maker of Heaven and earth and in Jesus Christ, His only Son our Lord who was conceived by the Holy Spirit, born of the Virgin Mary, suffered under Pontius Pilate, was crucified, dead and buried. The third day He arose from the dead; He ascended into heaven and sitteth at the right hand of God the Father Almighty: from thence He shall come to judge the quick and the dead. I believe in the Holy Spirit, the Church Universal, the communion of saints, the forgiveness of sins, the resurrection of the body and the life everlasting.

Confirmands: All this I truly believe.

Let us Pray: God of grace, God of mercy, I present unto you these your children who have successfully completed their confirmation course. Each of them has a desire to be one with you in the kingdom of God. Consecrate them now by the power of your Holy Spirit so that they may serve you well, live well and manage their lives well. Anoint them with your presence by the power of grace divine. Equip them and protect them with your Word so they will be able to withstand the attacks of the enemy. Give them strength, wisdom and knowledge to be more than conquerors over every trial and temptation. Give them discernment to make the right choices in all their endeavors, through Jesus Christ our Lord. Amen.

Pastor: I present to you (name your church) these confirmands. May the Spirit and the grace of God be with you now and forevermore!

"...You are a part of the body of Christ.
God has chosen different ones in the church to do his work."
1 Corinthians 12:27-28

BIBILOGRAPHY

Barbour, Johnny Jr. *African Methodist Episcopal Church Hymnal* Nashville, TN: African Methodist Episcopal Church. 2000.

Elwell, Walter A., and Philip Wesley Comfort. *Tyndale Bible Dictionary.* Tyndale reference library. Wheaton, Ill: Tyndale House Publishers, 2001.

http://www.ame-church.com AMEC Administered by the General Secretary/Chief Information Officer, 2011.

McKim, Donald K., *Westminster Dictionary of Theological Terms;* Westminster John Knox Press Louisville, 1996.

Moltmann, Jurgen. *The Way of Jesus Christ: Christology in Messianic Dimensions.* Minneapolis, MI: Fortress Press, 1993.

Morgan, Robert J. *Then Sings My Soul.* Nashville, TN, Thomas Nelson Publishers. 2003.

The Doctrine and Discipline of the African Methodist Episcopal Church. Forty-seventh Ed. Nashville, TN: The AMEC Sunday School Union, 2005.

The Holy Bible, *Teen Devotional Bible, New International Version.* Grand Rapids, MI: Zondervan Publishing, 1999.

Zinkiewicz, Crystal A. *Claim the Name: Confirmation Plans for 8 Weeks.* Nashville, TN: Cokesbury, 2005.

"...You are a part of the body of Christ.
God has chosen different ones in the church to do his work."
1 Corinthians 12:27-28

105

ENDNOTES

1. The Holy Bible, *Teen Devotional Bible, New International Version.* Grand Rapids, MI: Zondervan, p. 1475

2. W. A. Elwell & P.W. Comfort, Tyndale Bible Dictionary, (Wheaton: Tyndale House Publishers, 2001), p. 1275.

3. Crystal A. Zinkiewicz, Claim the Name: Confirmation Plans for 8 Weeks (Nashville: Cokesbury, 2005), p. 31.

4. Donald K. McKim, *Westminster Dictionary of Theological Terms;* Westminster John Knox Press Louisville, p.218.

5. Robert J. Morgan, Then Sings My Soul; Thomas Nelson Publishers. Nashville, p. xi

6. ibid., p. 20

7. African Methodist Episcopal Church Hymnal, p. 798.

8. The Book of Discipline of The African Methodist Episcopal Church, AMEC Publishing House. Nashville, p.16

9. ibid., p. 16.

10. ibid., p. 16.

11. ibid., p. 18.

12. ibid., p. 18.

13. ibid., p. 18.

14. ibid., p. 19.

15. ibid., p. 20.

16. ibid., p. 20.

17. W. A. Elwell & P.W. Comfort. p. 1275.

"...You are a part of the body of Christ.
God has chosen different ones in the church to do his work."
1 Corinthians 12:27-28

107